Always Remember,

Your Story is Still Being Written . . .

Crystal Gilpin Jones

Always Remember,
Your Story is Still Being Written...
Crystal Gilpin Jones

Published August 2023
Express Editions
Imprint of Jan-Carol Publishing, Inc.

ISBN: 978-1-954978-96-6
Library of Congress Control Number: 2023943079

Jan-Carol Publishing, Inc
PO Box 701
Johnson City, TN 37605
publisher@jancarolpublishing.com
www.jancarolpublishing.com

To my brother and sister, who left us way too soon,
not all superheroes wear capes.

To my husband, daughter, and son
who always encouraged me in whatever I attempted.

To Susan, for encouraging me to proceed with this book.

To Uncle Joe, a true Godly example of love and compassion,
you are missed.

Foreword

By Varita H. Powers
Ocala, Florida

It's known that the music of David soothed the soul of King Saul and gave him rest in his spirit. In this day and age we live in, we all, no matter who we are, look for rest in our spirit and soothing for our minds. We don't always have the time for lengthy studies, as we rush off to begin our day, however, we can take a few minutes to give ourselves the boost we need to face the day.

I have found myself encouraged, uplifted, and reminded of the love of our great God as I have absorbed the words of Crystal's daily devotions. Words have power, especially when they come from the heart of a loving God, through His servant's heart to us. Be blessed and refreshed as you read the wonderfully written words of my dear sister and friend.

Author's Note

It is truly my desire the individual reader finds hope for whatever situation they may find themselves going through.

Always Remember,
Your Story is Still Being Written...

ALWAYS REMEMBER,

Your Story is
Still Being Written...

January

JANUARY 1

This is my prayer, for all of us: Lord Jesus, Today as I face down my giants, I declare that You are the One who fights for me. You bring the victory. You lead me to high places where I can see things from Your perspective. I trust You today. I will follow where You lead. I'll say what You tell me to say. Overwhelming victory is mine because I am Yours! I stand strong because You're strong in me. Amen!

JANUARY 2

Take your cues from God (and not from culture), and become a powerful, praying saint. Pray those prayers that make your knees buckle and your heart tremble as you entrust your whole soul and story to the God of the Universe. When the enemy comes in like a flood, the Lord raises a standard against him. This is no time for cowering in fear. This is a time to rise up in faith. Trust God's Word. Believe His promises. Do what He says. And in due time, you'll see the waters part, the mountains move, and the answers you've been waiting for. You are mighty in God. Enjoy deep, faith-filled assurance today and every day! He's always with you.

January 3

May God fine tune your spiritual ears, so you hear heaven's song above the chaos and the noise. May you rest in the knowledge that God is in control and will have the last say when it's all said and done. Though the elements rage and the enemy taunts, God is the One who fights for you, and He will win for you. He loves you with power and with passion. May His Kingdom come, and His will be done everywhere you place your feet today. You can have a powerful day in Him.

January 4

May you find a new freedom in being the "you" God created you to be. May you be comfortable in your own skin, excited about your own story, and at peace with your own past because Christ has redeemed every part of you. God's love breaks you free from condemnation, and you can walk away from toxic influences, and put your fear under your feet. Let faith fill your heart. Do not give people the power that belongs to God alone. He loves you. He is strong. And He'll keep you strong 'till the end. Have a faith-filled day.

January 5

May Jesus lift your chin today and speak life into your weary soul. Feel afresh by remembering how much He loves you. May your bumps and the bruises be healed in His presence. Shake off today's frustrations and tomorrow's worries and rest in the reality of His divine involvement in your life. Jesus is more than enough for you. Listen for His life-giving invitation to you. He invites you to rest with Him. Trust Him and choose joy as you walk one step at a time.

JANUARY 6

May you open your hands and trust your cares to God. Be assured of this: Jesus knows your name, has your address, and loves who you are. He will get you where you need to go. He will reach out to the ones you love. He will validate and vindicate you at the proper time, all you have to do is hold on, stand and watch. Feel the comfort and know you're safest when you're at His feet, trusting Him to do what you cannot do for yourself. Allow your soul, spirit, mind, will and emotions to find rest in Him today.

JANUARY 7

May God answer your accumulative prayers for those you love. Draw nearby His Spirit. May He heal their deepest wounds, restore their perspective, make their crooked ways straight, and open their eyes where they're blind. May God Himself drive a wedge between every person and circumstance that the enemy is using to lie to and distract your loved ones from God's best for them. He moves when we pray. Rest in the promise that God loves your loved one far more passionately than you do. Choose joy and seek His wisdom through prayers. May your prayers take on a whole new level of power and faith.

JANUARY 8

May God do a brand-new thing in and through you. May He break every generational stronghold that keeps you from knowing and experiencing His great love for you. May He move every mountain that blocks your view of Him. May He fill every low place with pools of blessings. Allow Him to restore everything stolen so you can have the life He intended for you from the beginning of time. Your Redeemer is strong and mighty, and He loves you deeply. Live joyfully today!

JANUARY 9

Put a high priority on rest and replenishment. May you make a plan to get away and nourish your soul. Do your work with great excellence. Take on a challenge that stretches your faith and increases your dependence on God. Allow your work to be especially satisfying and your rest to be especially sweet. Life is good that way.

JANUARY 10

In this world of chaos, your small act of kindness may be a life-changing moment for someone. Try a small act each day...let someone over in your lane; let someone in front of you in line; smile with your eyes; keep the hand off the horn; tip your server (with cash and not a quote or track); sincerely thank the delivery person; call someone by name; and a hundred other ways. Just be kind. What may seem insignificant to you may mean the world to others. Be a positive ripple of change. Create a ripple of positivity for someone.

JANUARY 11

When life knocks you down, may you get back up again because greater is He who is in you than he who is in the world. When your rogue emotions turn you upside down, may you find your footing again by standing on the truth of who you are in Christ Jesus. When your perspective dims because the clouds block the sun, allow God Himself break through with a fresh perspective on His promises. You are loved, called, cared for, and appointed to be a blessing to a world very much in need. May the changeable things in your life take a back seat to the unchangeable, never-ending love and faithfulness of God. You're blessed and God has given you a sturdy place to stand.

JANUARY 12

May the reality of heaven mean more to you than your temporary circumstances on earth. Allow the promise of God's provision compel you to live generously and with expectancy. May you refrain from making long-term decisions based on short-term circumstances. Seek the blessings in your battles, tough as they are. Are you stronger because of them? Do you have more compassion for those who suffer because of the way you have suffered? Even in hardship, Jesus meets us, refines us, and empowers us to change the world. Refuse to get tangled up in your regrets from yesterday, your frustrations today, and your fears about tomorrow. Instead, lift your eyes and look to Jesus and live with eternity in mind. Today is the day to have a blessed, magnificent, eternally minded day.

JANUARY 13

My prayer for you is that God abundantly increase your capacity to walk with Him. May His power and His promises impact your every word and every step. Feel His increase in your territory, establish your influence, and awaken your faith. May He deepen your love, broaden your perspective, and increase your compassion. In every way, know God's redeeming, restorative, refreshing and renewing power in your life. Humility and holy spiritual momentum can be yours. Walk forward in faith today. In everything you do, be kind.

January 14

May you refuse condemnation for the ways you fail and fall short in your everyday life. May you instead, embrace God's relentless grace that covers you from head to toe. May you dare to entrust your whole soul and story to Jesus so you can fully enjoy your journey with Him. He's not disgusted by your weaknesses, He's moved by them, and He treasures you. Shake off your regrets and grab a firm hold of God's promise to forgive, restore, and renew your story. May others' opinions no longer tie you up in knots because God's opinion continually sets you free! Determine—with all your heart—to live the abundant, powerful, forgiven life Jesus has offered you. Lean into the soul-stirring, heart-freeing grace that Jesus purchased just for you. Be fully assured, Jesus has you close to His heart.

January 15

May you pause today, step back for a moment, and look above your disappointments, hurts, and heartaches. Do you see Jesus in this place? He is with you, for you, and will surely sustain you. He intends to strengthen your faith, sturdy your frame, and stir up a fresh passion for His Name. He is stronger than your fears, greater than your hurts, and deeper than your insecurities. And He has you in His hand. You're strong in Him, safe with Him, and established because of Him. May Jesus open a window of heaven and give you a glimpse of who you are because you're His. He sings over you and in due time, He will deliver you. A renewed perspective can be yours today.

JANUARY 16

May God answer your accumulative prayers for those you love. May He draw them nearby His Spirit. May He heal their deepest wounds, restore their perspective, make their crooked ways straight, and open their eyes where they're blind. May God Himself drive a wedge between every person and circumstance that the enemy is using to lie to and distract your loved ones from God's best for them.

JANUARY 17

May He line your path with people and circumstances that speak life-giving, soul-restoring truth until all are totally free! May a revival break out, may the prodigals come home, may the weary be restored, and the broken be healed. We wait together for God to do what only He can do. He moves when we pray. Rest in the promise that God loves your loved one far more passionately than you do! Choose joy in the meantime.

JANUARY 18

No matter what you're going through, you can know, in the depths of your soul, that you are loved. Your identity is completely secure. It's not up for grabs or changeable with popular opinion. Jesus is sold on the idea of you and loves how He made you. Seasons come and seasons go, but God's love for you never changes. It's abundant, profound, and amazingly real, right here, right now. Walk like you're loved because you are beyond your wildest dreams. Have a beautiful day in Him.

JANUARY 19

May God remove every hindrance that keeps you from knowing His love changing you into a new you. Seek His changes in every circumstance that sends a lying message to you. May He highlight every trial by His using it to train you to become a warrior. And may He remind you that all of Heaven is on your side. You are very close to His heart.

JANUARY 20

When you can't sense what God is up to, that is when you trust even more. His heart towards you. When your journey is different than you would choose, seek His invitation to make you new. When the storm rages overhead, may you know—with everything in you—that new mercies are on the other side. And when you're tempted to overstate your problems and understate His promises, step back and find your footing again. On Christ the solid rock you stand, all other ground is sinking sand. He is mighty to save, and He is doing a new and beautiful thing in you. Embrace a joy-perspective today!

JANUARY 21

May God open the heavens and pour a fresh grace awakening into your soul. May you understand—on a whole new level—what it means to rest in the finished work of Christ. Abound in every good work because God's grace empowers you. Persevere in prayer because His grace fuels you. Refuse to strive for appearance's sake because you've already been established for Jesus's namesake. You are loved, treasured, appointed, and anointed. You're free to climb mountain heights with joy and free to stumble and fall without condemnation. Jesus holds you and will lead you safely home. Have a heart-at-rest sort of day today!

JANUARY 22

Do you Love the sound of God's voice in your ear. May you nurture such a heart of peace and a heart at rest that you fully trust your God to lead you in the way that you should go. Turn away from the things that weaken you. Develop a hunger and a thirst for all God has for you. Seek a fresh revelation of God's love and promise for you. You are a gifted, treasured, loved person and you're called to impact the world in a way that only you can. Only the love of Christ can constrain you and compel you in the days ahead. Open your eyes to the new territory He has waiting for you.

JANUARY 23

May God, abundantly, increase your capacity to walk with Him. May His power and His promises impact your every word and every step. See His increase in your territory, establish your influence, and awaken your faith. May He deepen your love, broaden your perspective, and increase your compassion. In every way, may you know God's redeeming, restorative, refreshing, and renewing power in your life. May humility and holy spiritual momentum be yours. Walk forward in faith today.

JANUARY 24

Today, may God give you unprecedented clarity about His plans for you in the days ahead. May you find utter joy in His presence because

He fully enjoys you. When He sets the plow a little deeper in the soil of your character, may you refuse despair. Instead, know that in Christ there is never any condemnation, only an invitation. When God corrects and redirects it's because He's about to do a new thing. Listen with your heart. Do what He says by responding in faith. Trust that God's will for you is your best-case-scenario. Enjoy this day as a bright and beautiful day.

JANUARY 25

Make God's opinion more important to you than man's opinion. May His dreams for you speak louder than your fears. May you refuse to read into situations that make you anxious. Jesus's promise to protect and provide will be enough for you. Accept His forgiveness and let it wash over every sin from your past. Rise up in the knowledge that He's made you brand new, through and through. No spot or stain on you.

JANUARY 26

May the Lord Himself establish you in His highest and best purposes for you. May He open doors, move mountains, and bring provision in the very near future. May He confirm your faith steps and energize your prayers. He is mighty, He is good, and He cares about every detail of your life. Dare to obey Him and do what He says. He's making a way where there is no way. He loves you truly and deeply. Trust Him, in all things.

JANUARY 27

May you refuse condemnation for the ways you fail and fall short in your everyday life. Instead, embrace God's relentless grace that covers you from head to toe. Entrust your whole soul and story to Jesus so you can fully enjoy your journey with Him. He's not disgusted by your weaknesses, He's moved by them, and He treasures you. Shake off your regrets and grab a firm hold of God's promise to forgive, restore, and renew your story. Lean into the soul-stirring, heart-freeing grace that Jesus purchased just for you. Be fully assured, Jesus has you close to His heart.

JANUARY 28

May God surround you with a strong sense of His great love for you! Live every day with the expectancy that He is moving in your life. May the Word of God come alive to you in a way you've never experienced. May your prayers take on a whole new level of power and faith. You are His child, and He is with you every step of the way. Be blessed with deep peace and hope.

JANUARY 29

When you can't sense what God is up to, may you trust even more. When your journey is different than you would choose, may you see His invitation to make you new. When you see the storm rages overhead, know that new mercies are on the other side. When you're tempted to overstate your problems and understate His promises, take a step back and find your footing again. Christ is the solid rock you stand while all other ground is sinking sand. He is mighty to save. Embrace He is doing a new and beautiful thing in you. Seek joy for the day!

January 30

Today, in the midst of difficult situations, God wants us to know He has a plan. He also wants us to know as we submit to His plan that He desires to use us and to bless the world around us. The key still remains during both good and difficult times: You will seek Me and find Me when you search with your whole heart. Whatever comes your way...don't lose focus...don't lose hope. Always, remember your story is still being written.

January 31

May you grow to love and accept the YOU God is making you to be. May you walk in a new level of grace and gratitude that gives you peace and leaves others encouraged. May you be more apt to look forward with hope than you are to look back with regret. May your heart spill over with joy at the very thought of the story God is writing with your life.

Don't lose focus.

Don't lose hope.

Always remember,

your story is still being written.

Write Notes:

__/__/__

Write Notes:

__/__/__

February

FEBRUARY 1

May you pause today, step back for a moment, and look above your disappointments, hurts, and heartaches. Do you see Jesus in this place? He is with you, for you, and will surely sustain you. He intends to strengthen your faith, sturdy your frame, and stir up a fresh passion for His name. He is stronger than your fears, greater than your hurts, and deeper than your insecurities. He has you in His hands. You're strong in Him, safe with Him, and established because of Him. May Jesus open a window of heaven and give you a glimpse of who you are because you're His. He sings over you and in due time, He will deliver you. A renewed perspective can be yours today!

FEBRUARY 2

May God give you startling clarity about His plans for you in the days ahead. May you find absolute joy in His presence because He fully enjoys you. When He sets the plow a little deeper in the soil of your character, you can refuse despair. Know that in Christ, there is never any condemnation, only an invitation. When God corrects and redirects, it's because He's about to do a NEW thing. So lean in. Listen with your heart. Do what He says. Respond in faith. And trust that God's will for you is your best-case-scenario. Have a bright and beautiful day!

FEBRUARY 3

May you dare to keep walking even though quitting feels like the easier thing to do. May you dare to look up even though the weight of your burden compels you to look down. May you dare to dream about the future even though the enemy would love for your past to have the last say. Keep walking, look up, and dare to dream. Jesus invites you forward. Never give up, even when it appears the darkest, He still has a plan.

FEBRUARY 4

Pilgrims Progress—one of the greatest pieces of literature, in my opinion, in history. It was written from a place of absolute hopelessness. *The Pilgrim's Progress: From This World to That Which Is to Come* is a 1678 Christian allegory written by John Bunyan.

Don't let your hearts be troubled, even in the middle of the most difficult situations, the middle of a hurricane, the middle of tornadoes, when lightning strikes over and over again and when it feels as if there is an onslaught of troubles. God is with us and has laid the road map for us. God is in control. None of the world's chaos takes Him by surprise. We must remember, He is still with us in our journey. He is with us in tragedy, illness and despair. God will see us through. He has a plan and a purpose. Don't give up and don't cave to the pressure. God has already made a way for us to be victorious. Be assured, He has made you and He will not leave you alone on your journey.

February 5

Over the years I've seen many different bumper stickers. I've seen one indicating the world is hopeless, another "Hope is Real." I began to think about these words, after hearing a young mother lost her third child to the same ugly dreaded disease of cancer. Then Eddie James's song, "I AM" resonated through my mind. Hope is very REAL. I thought about it and needless to say agreed with the statement Hope is Real. As I pondered that little phrase, I realized for many, hope is not real. I believe one of the most important gifts we can give another person, the gift of Hope.

February 6

Someone who is hopeless and alone usually cannot help themselves out of their situation. They have a great sense of helplessness and loss. We must come alongside and bring the good news of Jesus Christ and all that He has to offer. One definition for hope is: to look forward with confidence or expectation. We must bring the Word of God with all its hope to someone who does not know it is real. When we bring hope, we bring life.

FEBRUARY 7

"For I know the plans I have for you," declares the Lord, "plans to prosper you and not to harm you, plans to give you hope and a future." Jeremiah 29:11 New International Version (NIV)

It's very easy when thinking about God's plan for our lives to have the attitude, "it's all about me." Yes, it's true that God cares about every intricate detail in our lives. In fact, Jesus said that even the hairs on our heads are numbered. We can also mistakenly think that God's plan is always going to be a 'feel good' plan with the intent to make us happy. Jeremiah's message in these verses is actually radically different. He's writing to a group of people who are being held captive and are in exile from their homeland. He's writing to let them know that although they're not where they would have expected, nor where they would have asked God to place them, God has not forgotten them, and He still has a plan for their lives. Even in the midst of a difficult situation, God wants them to know His plans.

In the preceding verses we see that a big part of God's plan is for them to "seek the welfare of the city where I have sent you into exile." (Jeremiah 29:7)

In other words, God wants them to know that His plans are not just to benefit them personally. God is also telling them that He is not removing them from the situation immediately. He does promise to eventually restore them, but it's not coming quickly (70 years out when many of them will be dead). God is letting them know they can move forward, because in the eternal picture, God's justice will prevail, and everything will even out.

In the midst of difficult situations, God wants us to know He has a plan. He also wants us to know that as we submit to His plan that

He desires to use us to bless the world around us. The key still remains during both good and difficult times: You will seek Me and find Me when you search for Me with all your heart.

FEBRUARY 8

In this next season may it be one of Affirmation of your Worth and Acceptance of your Uniqueness. May you be admired for just being you and experience the Love of God in your most trying circumstances. Find peace and bear fruit where's there's only been anxiety, fear and troublesome-prickly-thorns. May you experience a personal revival that changes how you pray, what you say, and where you put your time. Seek to experience such soul renewal that even the old things in your life feel new. Seek to experience fresh relationships and even love. God doesn't make things "nice"; He makes things new. Trust Him to do a brand-new work in you in the days ahead.

FEBRUARY 9

May we realize our tears, our pain, our suffering, our heartbreak is nothing new to the ages of life. Yet, we have a hope in Christ Jesus that gives us the assurance He is with us in our suffering, He is capturing our tears, He comforts us in our heartbreak, He gives us strength through our suffering, He heals our pain, He causes our tragedies to become triumphs. Why do we go through these things? How long do we have to suffer? What did I do to cause this? Have we been forgotten? Have we been forsaken? A resounding NO...we are still His and He has us in the palm of His hand. There will be beauty rising from the ashes; hope rises from the pain; strength comes from suffering. Hold on, hold strong, hold fast, dig deep, and hold to Him. When we can't see His hand...trust His heart.

FEBRUARY 10

Have you ever seen someone fall or possibly fallen yourself ? Have your feet ever tangled in a rug, and you did a dance attempting to stay upright? Have you ever grabbed something to keep from falling? We all have. What about a life-altering event coming from nowhere? No one expects the rug to be yanked out from under them; life-changing events usually don't announce themselves. Not one person thought that would be their last. While instinct and intuition can help provide some warning signs, they can do little to prepare you for a feeling of rootlessness that follows when fate flips your world upside down. Anger, confusion, sadness, and frustration are shaken up together inside you like a snow-globe. It takes years for the emotional dust to settle as you do your best just to see through the storm. Daily, we are on a journey of hope and life. Yet, in a moment the unimaginable can unfold. All we can do is hold to His word, His hand, and trust Him. Whatever life brings, He is still with us.

FEBRUARY 11

May God fine-tune your spiritual ears, so you hear heaven's song above the chaos and the noise. Rest in the knowledge that God is in control and will have the last say when it's all said and done. Though the elements rage and the enemy taunts, God is the One who fights for you, and He will win for you. He loves you with power and with passion. May His Kingdom come, and His will be done everywhere you place your feet today. Have a powerful day in Him.

FEBRUARY 12

Isn't life changing to believe in something? To see hope at the end of a long, dark tunnel? Hope is more than just asking God for something we are so badly needing. We must expect our miracle. Somewhere in the middle of asking, believing, and expecting God to answer, we will find what we are looking for. We can look around and see hopelessness on faces, in body language. There are so many hurts, problems, sicknesses, troubles, financial woes, world issues, political concerns, etc. It seems the world has no hope. But, with God our troubles vanish. The problem may still exist, but the HOPE has been revived. May you allow God to breathe hope into your heart and life today.

FEBRUARY 13

Have you ever felt disappointed? Have you ever felt alone? Today, may you feel His presence, may you feel His reassurance. May today be the day, encouragement in His word prevails over the whispers the enemy is trying to put inside your ear and heart. You are an overcomer. You are more than a conqueror. You are precious in His eyes. He has you and He has your best interests at heart. Wrap your arms around yourself, give yourself a great big God hug, He is holding you. He is with you.

FEBRUARY 14

May the Lord awaken you to fresh and powerful revelations of His love. May He stir in you a deep desire to read His word and stand on His promises. Allow Him to lift you up so you can see your life from His perspective. Feel His joy in your heart that makes you glad and others smile. Today, wrap yourself up in this wonderful truth: Absolutely nothing can separate you from His love.

February 15

May you see the value of the gifts God has given you. May you see the importance of your contribution in the world today. Get excited about your role in the greater Kingdom story. Dare to dream with God about the ways He intends to use you in the days ahead. You're living and breathing on the earth today because God loves you, has called you, and intends to solve some of the world's problems through you. Embrace the fact that you're a treasure and enjoy sweet peace today.

February 16

When life knocks you down, may you have the courage to get back up again because greater is He who is in you than he who is in the world! When your rogue emotions turn you upside down, may you find your footing again by standing on the truth of who you are in Christ Jesus. When your perspective dims because the clouds block the sun, may God Himself break through with a fresh perspective on His promises. Even here, right in this place, you are loved, called, cared for, and appointed to be a blessing to a world very much in need. May the changeable things in your life take a back seat to the unchangeable, never-ending love and faithfulness of God. You're blessed and God has given you a sturdy place to stand. Today is the day to have a great day.

FEBRUARY 17

May you abound in spiritual discernment in the days ahead! May you know when God is asking you to shore up your faith and stand strong, and when He's inviting you hide yourself under the shadow of His wing. May you quickly discern the enemy's schemes and stay clear of the traps he sets for you. In spite of your mistakes, missteps, and misunderstandings, you never have to doubt your worth and your value. You're someone God loves, treasures, anoints, and appoints. He'll show Himself strong in your weakness, faithful in your fears, and merciful where you fall short. Walk wisely with Him today. There's a best place, a best path for your feet. Take every step with Jesus today. Have a wise, discerning day!

FEBRUARY 18

May God grant you a fresh perspective of His unlimited supply. May you trust Him with your needs and desires. Accept His breath of fresh life into your soul and fresh power into your dreams. May you refuse to let your fears and insecurities speak louder than God's voice. Even as you go about your busy day, allow your ears be fine-tuned to Heaven's song over you, for it is redemptive, beautiful, and live giving!

FEBRUARY 19

Sometimes God wants to shut a door completely before He can open doors to new possibilities. Maybe you have had some doors closed in your life. In spite of everything, know that God is stirring you to accomplish His purpose in your life. God knows what it takes to bring order back to your life. Trust Him. He's working on something and when He's done, everything around you will be made better.

FEBRUARY 20

This past week, I observed a little girl crying at the bus stop. A boy and a girl walked up to her, sat down and were just there for her. They apparently weren't related but knew each other well. I could hear their conversation telling the little girl crying, "it's okay, we will just sit and be with you." Isn't that how God is? When we are down, crying, and feeling overwhelmed...His Son and Spirit just come and are with us. No words necessary just their presence makes things seem less overwhelming. Trust Him.

FEBRUARY 21

Whatever is making you feel overwhelmed today. It is not taking Him by surprise. He knew this day before we woke up this morning. It's okay to sit in His presence and just be there. May we realize, we don't always have to be doing something. We are people who seem to always be on the go. Today, just sit in His presence, enjoy time with Him. It's okay. May we take a deep breath, inhale His goodness and enjoy the beauty of Who He is.

FEBRUARY 22

May you have a strong sense of the impossible things God wants to do in, through, and around you. Seek God's dream for you and swallow up your unbelief. Have faith enough to put out your buckets and prepare for rain. God moves on faith. He moves mightily because of your faith. Today, walk confidently knowing He has everything in control. God is mighty to save and mighty in all things.

February 23

May the reality of heaven mean more to you than your temporary circumstances on earth. The promise of God's provision can compel you to live generously and with expectancy. Open your eyes to see the blessings in your battles, tough as they are. Are you stronger because of them? Do you have more compassion for those who suffer because of the way you have suffered? Even in hardship, Jesus meets us, refines us, and empowers us to change the world. Refuse to get tangled up in your regrets from yesterday, your frustrations today, and your fears about tomorrow. Decide to lift your eyes and look to Jesus. Live with eternity in mind. Today, have a blessed, magnificent, eternally minded day!

February 24

May you stand strong in the face of enemy threats. May you remain confident even if an army rises up against you. Put your flag in the ground and declare that if God is for you, who can stand against you? Far greater is He who is in you, than he who is in the world. May you rise up on this day and walk forward in holy confidence and humble dependence. You are God's beloved child, and He will guard and guide you, shelter and provide for you, bless and establish you. Jesus loves you and nothing and no one can change His mind about you. He's sold on the idea of you, always. Live like you're His, because you are, and you can know this!

February 25

May the Holy Spirit detoxify your soul! May He show you what habits, thoughts, and actions need to go so the Lord can strengthen you for the road ahead. Sense the holy invitation before you. Get a glimpse of His plan for you; just enough to inspire you to make the necessary changes, take the necessary steps, and grab a firm hold of His promises. Are you willing to do something different, so you'll be ready and equipped for this next place of promise? He's got a new chapter ahead for you. Care enough about your story to leave the lesser things behind. You're so precious and important to Him! Enjoy His blessings on your day today.

February 26

May God remove every hindrance that keeps you from knowing His love in a way that changes you. Allow Him to change every circumstance that sends a lying message to you. He will highlight every trial He's using to train you into a warrior. He remind you that all of heaven is on your side. You are very close to His heart. He's got you. Today, live and breathe with expectancy and hope.

February 27

May you refuse to drag the heavy baggage from your past another step. Refuse to borrow tomorrow's trouble when it's not yours to carry. Grab hold of today's mercy, today's grace, and today's power offered you in this moment. Walk in the delegated influence God has assigned you. Walk in a manner worthy of His name. Today, may holy confidence and humble dependence mark your life in every way!

FEBRUARY 28

May you look around and notice all of the answers to prayers you enjoy because of prayers you prayed some time ago. Allow the breakthroughs you've experienced and the open doors you've walked through compel you to pray with more fervency, specificity, and tenacity. God loves your faith. He loves your heart. He loves it when you pray. He's very protective of you and won't give you something that's not good for you. He makes you wait because He's making you ready. Trust your whole soul and story to Him. And keep praying. God is moving, even when you can't see it. Make today a blessed, beautiful, and prayerful day!

DON'T LOSE FOCUS.

DON'T LOSE HOPE.

ALWAYS REMEMBER,

YOUR STORY IS STILL BEING WRITTEN.

Write Notes:

__/__/__

March

MARCH 1

When you're weary and tired, may God give you rest and a right perspective. When you long to run ahead on your own, may He give you divine wisdom to wait on Him. When your guard is down and you're vulnerable to the enemy's schemes, accept that God protects you and delivers you on every side. And when you're ready to fly, may He lift you up and bless you before a watching world. Take one humble step at a time. He'll lead you to your next place of promise. May yours be a powerful, nourishing, faith-filled day!

MARCH 2

May you refuse to drag your past with you another step. May you stop right here, stomp your feet, and raise your hands in the air because Christ has set you free! He has redeemed you, received you, and claimed you for His purposes! He has forgiven you and filled you anew with His powerful Holy Spirit. There is "now no" condemnation for you because you are in Him and He is in you. May you walk free and full of grace—even amidst your weaknesses and frailties—because He's got you. You get to be a work in progress, and you are a masterpiece because He says so. Rejoice in His goodness today because you're one of the good gifts He offers to a world very much in need. Bless your day today!

MARCH 3

May the wonder of Christ's love and the miracle of His redemption sweep you off your feet and ignite your faith once again. May you dare to look away from your discouragements and look toward your Deliverer who truly makes all things new. May your heart of faith beat once again for the promises God has made to you. May you pick up the cause of faith and march forward knowing God has your back, He's gone before you, and He's placed His hand of blessing upon your head (Psalm 139:5). Awaken to joy today! Embrace faith today! Pray like you have a God in heaven who hears you and moves when you pray... because you do! Have a blessed and beautiful day this day.

MARCH 4

Has your tired become tired? Has your weary gotten so weary it can't put one foot in front of the other? This world is in chaos, yet...God is still in control. Even when our tiredness and weariness is overwhelming us. Have we ever thought our tiredness and weariness are more because of the spiritual battles we can't see, which is affecting our physical? I have heard so many times when fatigue walks in faith walks out. It is true, when we are so weary and fatigued, it is hard to have faith. But deep down we know God is still in control and He has us in the palm of His hand. So, when your tired is tired and your weary is overwhelming...don't give up, turn your face to Him. It's okay to say no, it's okay to rest yourself, it's okay to refresh your spirit and soul on this day!

MARCH 5

May you turn your situation over to God. He can do more in a moment than you can do in a lifetime. Your situation does not take Him by surprise. He has you and He is your answer. When you don't know which way to turn, turn to Him. You are His and He is yours. There are deposits of wealth and gifts on the inside of you, waiting to grow and be cultivated. May you not allow your situation to stop all God has for you.

MARCH 6

Speak encouragement to someone today. May you allow God to help you be a restorer. In the world, we hear negative all around us. We are constantly bombarded by the barrage of should've, could've, would've. No one knows what it took for you to make the choice you did today. We don't know others' stories and why they chose the path they did. Be an encourager, a restorer, a lifter up. Be the person who makes a difference by making others feel better about themselves.

MARCH 7

No matter if you're in the valley or on a mountain, may you remember most importantly that as a Christ-follower you are seated with Christ in the heavenly realms. Everything He has is yours. He's written your name on His hand and holds your desires close to His heart. Though the elements rage on earth, your footing is secure in Him. Stay hidden in the shelter of His wing; stay in that place of peace. Nothing can separate you from His powerful, personal love for you. You're everything to Him. Remember His love today!

MARCH 8

When life knocks you down, may you get back up again because greater is He who is in you than he who is in the world! When your rogue emotions turn you upside down, may you find your footing again by standing on the truth of who you are in Christ Jesus. When your perspective dims because the clouds block the sun, may God Himself break through with a fresh perspective on His promises. Even here, right in this place, you are loved, called, cared for, and appointed to be a blessing to a world very much in need. May the changeable things in your life take a back seat to the unchangeable, never-ending love and faithfulness of God. You're blessed and God has given you a sturdy place to stand. Have a great joyful day!

MARCH 9

When you look in the mirror today, may you see the beautiful you who God sees. He sees a wonderfully made creation. When we realize who we are in Him, we can be all He intends for us to be in every area of our lives. We can experience Him in a new and different way when we realize just how beautiful we are. When we look in that mirror and realize we are made in His image, we can see ourselves and others in a different light.

MARCH 10

May you find shelter beneath the shadow of God's wing. May you be wise enough to stay in His established space for you, trusting He'll move you to your next place when the timing is right. May His grace empower you to live abundantly, to stand strong, and to pray powerfully. May your honor for Him compel you to trust Him when your trials seem truer than His word. He will not fail you, will not forget about you, and will not turn away from you. He's with you in battle, He'll help you when your heart breaks, and He'll deliver you and bless you before a watching world when the time is right. Trust Him. You're so very dear to His heart. Have a grace-filled day.

MARCH 11

When you feel like you don't fit in, may you walk in faith because you have a place at the Table of Grace. When you feel like you're just not enough, may you remember that His Enough is more than enough for you. When people attempt to make you feel less than, insignificant, unimportant, remember to Whom you belong. He didn't make a mistake when He created you. When you trip up and fall short, remember that He stoops down to make you great. And when you don't feel victorious, remember that you're already seated with Christ because He won the victory for you. Have a great day!

MARCH 12

May you find rest in Him alone. When our emotions are in turmoil and we're waiting on the answer to prayers, it doesn't appear anything is going right. May we remember, He is working on our behalf even when we can't see His hand. When we can't see His hand, Trust His heart. May you be reminded that He is your source.

MARCH 13

May today be the day you dare to sing a new song unto him, even when your heart is heavy and burdened. May you slow down and sit for a while, just for a little rest and meditation. When you stand, stand firm and strong resolving to rely on His word and promises. All it takes is one step at a time to walk forward in faith. Remember, He has your back and He has your future.

MARCH 14

As the winds of change start to blow in your life, may you lean in and listen for the voice of the Lord. Instead of looking for 'signs' and mistakenly drawing the wrong conclusion, may you instead look to the Lord and His strength. He'll speak to you in a way you'll understand. He'll lead you in the way you should go. He is faithful and true and He's doing a "new" thing in your life! Keep your ear bent toward heaven. Daily the heavens pour forth speech. May you listen for every word. Blessings on your day today!

MARCH 15

May you divinely discern the difference between holy conviction and unholy condemnation. May you walk wisely without walking in fear. May you guard your heart without closing it off and shutting it down. Learn to live freely, wisely, and full of faith in spite of the enemy's attempts to bait you into fear and captivity. You are a royal ambassador of the Most High God. When life throws you a curve ball, may you allow God to coach you into turning it into a home run. May holy confidence and humble dependence mark your life in every way and may God's richest blessings be yours, today and every day.

MARCH 16

May you look up and remember once again that the Lord is your very dear and precious Shepherd. Because you have Him, you have everything you need. He causes you to lie down and rest, He leads you to still waters and sacred spaces to restore your soul. He leads you along His best path for your life for His namesake. Even when you walk through the deepest valley, He is right there with you, close beside you. He corrects and directs, guides and provides, and He'll never forsake you. He establishes you and honors you in front of your enemies. He pours out a fresh anointing on your life when you need it. He fills your cup to overflowing. His goodness and mercy chase after you and always will. You are blessed because you get to dwell in the house of the Lord all the days of your life. Have a sacred-paced-heart-at-rest kind of day. He's got you!

MARCH 17

May you choose to be grateful when it's easier to be grumpy. May you choose to rejoice in God's goodness when you're tempted to focus on people's badness. Never allow others negativity to be your constant diet. Sometimes you must remove yourself from the negativity that surrounds and embodies some on a constant basis. Life is too short; the journey is never easy...but God. Laugh until it hurts. God gave us that ability for a reason. Sing into your empty well, trusting that God will soon fill it. And may you live with the expectation that any day now, the Lord will bring the breakthrough. Be assured in the knowledge that more rests on God's shoulders than on yours. He's got you.

MARCH 18

May God ignite fresh faith in you today! May you pray with clarity, precision, and power. May you stand on His word and hold fast to His promises. May you refuse to fixate on your difficulties and instead fix your eyes on Jesus—the One who will finish what He started in you! When things look more negative than positive, be assured appearances can be deceiving. God is still in control, and He knows what He's doing. During these overwhelmingly difficult and trying times, may you focus on kindness and not self-absorption. May we remind ourselves, He is always good, always kind, and always true, and He will come through for you! May the Lord overwhelm you with an awakening of faith, hope, and love today. Look up and be blessed on this day!

MARCH 19

If one life shines, the one next to it will catch the light. May you always keep your light shining so others may see Jesus through you. It isn't easy, but it is worth it when we stay humble before Him. Just like a fire draws others for warmth on a cold winter day, our light will draw others to a knowledge of Him. When we live a life of light-giving-warmth, He will bless us by bringing others to Him.

MARCH 20

May we always remember when we are apart from God it is an awful hopeless place. I want you to know whatever circumstance that makes you think you're too far gone; you are not. There is always hope in Him. You may not be able to feel, see, or hear...but there is hope. How do we find hope? There is only one place can be found and that is in Jesus Christ.

MARCH 21

May you become an expert at caring for your soul. May you know when to tuck yourself under the shadow of God's wing and when to run to the battle line, knowing He'll fight for you. May you know when to rest and know when to work. Refuse worry and embrace faith. May you become tenacious when it comes to the promises of God and tender when you think about His love for you. Guard against toxic thoughts, attitudes, and mindsets that only weaken you. May you instead, fill your thoughts with all that's lovely, praiseworthy, and true. In the days ahead, may your intimate walk with Jesus inform your decisions, fuel your prayers, and magnify your love. May Jesus fill you up to overflowing from one moment to the next. Have a wise and wonderful day.

MARCH 22

May we stand in faith, praying, and believing: "Father in Heaven, I lift my eyes to You. Fill us fresh with Your Holy Spirit. Turn over the hardened soil in our lives and plant something fresh and beautiful there! Help us with a new measure of faith, so we can trust You with more of our lives. Open eyes to see Your movement all around. During the most difficult time some of us have ever encountered, may we refuse discouragement and disappointment. May we embrace courage and the divine appointments You have for us today. May we realize kindness is a free gift we can give to others. May our lives be a witness of Your goodness and provision. Help us to walk in a manner worthy of our calling, and worthy Your Name." Amen!

MARCH 23

May the Lord Himself give you a fresh perspective on your life. May you begin to see your troubles—tough as they are—as momentary. Wrap your arms around the promise that those very troubles are achieving for you, an eternal glory that far outweighs them all. Jesus is deeply invested in your journey and doesn't intend to leave you stranded. He goes before you, He has your back, and He puts His hand of blessing upon your head. When appearance deceive and you think you stand alone, He is always by your side. May He give you a glimpse of glory, a peek into the eternal significance of your life because He is doing glorious work in and through you! You matter deeply to Him. May your spirit be renewed in His presence today!

MARCH 24

May God wildly increase your capacity to walk with Him. May His power and His promises impact your every word and every step. He will increase your territory, establish your influence, and awaken your faith. He will deepen your love, broaden your perspective, and multiply your compassion. In every way, may you know God's redeeming, multiplying power in your life. May humble and holy spiritual momentum be yours. Walk forward in faith today, being confident in His ability to take care of the smallest details of your life.

MARCH 25

May God prove Himself strong on your behalf. May He show you how to wisely and strategically stand in this place. Raise your shield of faith and block every fiery arrow the enemy sends your way. Point your sword and dismantle every enemy scheme fashioned against you. May you know God's loving and intimate presence right here, right now, today. And may you experience firsthand how mighty, how powerful, and how faithful He truly is. God is mighty to save, He's with you in battle, and He's equipped you to win. Experience a blessed and joyful day, even in the middle of this horrible divisiveness raging across our world. When we see wars and hear rumors of wars, look up and see He is still with us and will never fail us. May we be assured; God is still in control and our source!

MARCH 26

I did a word search for "hope." I found many wonderful scriptures, mostly in Psalms and Proverbs. The folks in the Word had to remind themselves, many times, there is hope. No matter the situations, God always showed himself mighty on their behalf. Hope is real. Hope can be experienced. Hope can be felt, and hope can be seen. Trust God. He wants you to trust Him. May you realize, it can be as simple as just talking with Him. That's where hope is found.

MARCH 27

May you—above all else—see yourself as someone Jesus loves. His affection for you will heal you in the deepest ways and inspire you like nothing else ever has. Allow His saving grace and enabling power to compel you to dream with Him, believe in Him, and take crazy-faith-steps because of Him. Seek to have every lesser voice and every lying circumstance fall by the wayside so that all you hear is His voice in your ear saying, "This is the way, walk in it." Nobody's opinion matters as much as God's. Nobody can save, heal, redeem, and refresh like Jesus. Walk intimately with Him today. His will for you is your best-case-scenario.

MARCH 28

May you—above all else—see yourself as someone Jesus loves. May His affection for you heal you in the deepest ways and inspire you like nothing else ever has. Allow His saving grace and enabling power to compel you to dream with Him, believe in Him, and take crazy-faith-steps because of Him. May every lesser voice and every lying circumstance fall by the wayside so that all you hear is His voice in your ear saying, "This is the way, walk in it." Nobody's opinion matters as much as God's. Nobody can save, heal, redeem, and refresh like Jesus. Walk intimately with Him today. His will for you is your best-case-scenario. See yourself as someone Jesus loves, today!

MARCH 29

May you raise your shield of faith, draw a line in the sand, tell that enemy of your soul, "No more! You will steal from me no longer!" Refuse to be bullied by your fears. Don't put up with the enemy's taunts and threats. Put him under your feet where he belongs. Remember the authority you have in Christ. Pray God's Word with all the passion in your soul. Raise your shield and lift your voice. Embrace feisty, fearless, faith today. God has made you an overcomer!

MARCH 30

May you start and end your day with thoughts of God's goodness. May you, right here, right now, lift your hands and praise Jesus for the many blessings you enjoy! He came to earth to save you. He promised He'd never leave you. Do you have water to drink, clothes to wear, food to eat, and people to love? You have the promise of heaven and a purpose to fulfill. You have the Father, Son, and the Holy Spirit. You have freedom, possessions, and wisdom from above. You're richer than you know and more blessed than you can fathom. Live like you're loved and blessed, because you really, truly are! The "big" question is, do you settle for what you get? Or do you strive for what you want? Depends how bad you want it. The choice is yours. Never settle for an Ishmael when God has promised an Isaac.

MARCH 31

May the phrase "let go and let God" take on a whole new meaning for you. May you learn to rest while He works on your behalf. May you understand your role in this Kingdom story and do only what He tells you to do. Live free from the bondage of others' opinions so you're free to love them the way Christ does. May others be so drawn to your healed heart that they come to know Jesus for themselves. Unclench your fists, untangle your fears, and entrust your heart and story to the One who loves you deeply and cares for you profoundly. Let Him work while you rest. He's really good at what He does. Rest well in Him.

DON'T LOSE FOCUS.

DON'T LOSE HOPE.

ALWAYS REMEMBER,

YOUR STORY IS STILL BEING WRITTEN.

Write Notes:

__/__/__

April

APRIL 1

May God unearth the unsettled and unhealed places in your life so He can heal, renew, and restore you. Seek His reveal of a fresh revelation of His love and a new assurance of His grace. May He pour the oil of joy and gladness over your head and pools of blessing to splash your feet. Seek His unfathomable greatness so it may bring a fresh mystery and power to your prayers and perspective. Walk lightly today.

APRIL 2

May you find shelter beneath the shadow of God's wing. May you be wise enough to stay in His established space for you, trusting He'll move you to your next place when the timing is right. May His grace empower you to live abundantly, to stand strong, and to pray powerfully. Honor Him and it will compel you to trust Him when your trials seem truer than His word. He will not fail you, will not forget about you, and will not turn away from you. He's with you in battle, He'll help you when your heart breaks, and He'll deliver you and bless you before a watching world when the time is right. Trust Him. You're so very dear to His heart.

APRIL 3

As you walk forward to your next place of promise, may you refuse the bait of discouragement, offense, or fear. Instead, walk forward in faith, full of hope, and rich in love. Be so sensitive to God's voice that you rest when He says rest, and you run when He says run. He knows what's best for you and He'll get you where you need to go. Stay focused, prayerful, and hopeful. Though there are giants in the land, you have God on your side. Be brave. Be strong. Be courageous.

APRIL 4

May you look around and notice all of the answers to prayers. Enjoy because these prayers are prayers you prayed some time ago. Allow those breakthroughs you've experienced and the open doors you've walked through compel you to pray with more fervency, specificity, and tenacity. God loves your faith. He loves your heart. He loves it when you pray. He's very protective of you and won't give you something that's not good for you. He makes you wait because He's making you ready. Trust your whole soul and story to Him. And keep praying. God is moving, even when you can't see it. One day, your faith will become sight. Today is a blessed, beautiful, and prayerful day!

APRIL 5

May this next season for you be one of Rest, Revival, and Renewal. May you experience the rest of God in your most trying circumstances; and as a result, find peace and bear fruit where's there's only been anxiety, fear and troublesome-prickly-thorns. May you experience a personal revival that changes how you pray, what you say, and where you put your time. And may you experience such soul renewal that even the old things in your life feel new. God doesn't make things "nice." He makes things "new." Trust Him to do a brand-new work in you in the days ahead.

APRIL 6

Start your day with this prayer. Precious Lord, I lift my eyes to You tonight and ask for more of You in me! Shine a light in this dark world, open blind eyes, and set captives free. Many are lost, deceived, and confused. Many commit grievous sins in the name of religion. Only Your love heals. Only Your truth reveals the path of freedom. Awaken us to Your goodness, kindness, and clarity. You've appointed us to live in these desperate days; help us to love, live, and pray as ones who know You intimately and walk with You powerfully. May Your peace flow mightily in and through us. In Your Mighty and Matchless Name, I pray. Amen

APRIL 7

Scripture says that the SAME POWER that raised Christ from the dead is alive and available to us! May that very power quicken your mortal body, heal your deep soul wounds, and make you strong. May God's amazing love overwhelm you and fill you with a song. May His passion for the lost transform who you see and how you see them. May the promise of His provision and the access to His storehouses deeply impact how you give and live. We have reason to CELEBRATE every Easter Season! We serve a risen Christ; He's preparing a place for us; and He's coming again. Blessings on your day.

APRIL 8

May God do such a deep healing work in your soul that you're able to look at your disappointments and heartbreaks with a grounded sense of hope and perspective. May your emotions rest on God's immovable, abounding love and faithfulness. May you never again be tossed to and fro by the choices of others and the changes in your circumstances. Your rock is Christ and He is immovable. Stand on Him. Stand strong because of Him. And know this, one day He'll make your righteousness shine like the dawn and will reveal to the world that you belong to Him! Find your sturdy place of rest in Him today.

APRIL 9

As you walk forward to your next place of promise, may you refuse the bait of discouragement, offense, or fear. May you instead walk forward in faith, full of hope, and rich in love. May you be so sensitive to God's voice that you rest when He says rest, and you run when He says run. He knows what's best for you and He'll get you where you need to go. Stay focused, prayerful, and hopeful. Though there are giants in the land, you have God on your side. Be brave. Be strong. Be courageous. He's got you.

APRIL 10

May God Himself restore to you something you lost and never thought you'd get back again. Allow Him to heal a soul wound you thought you'd never get over. He will pour out an abundance of joy and hope that makes you celebrate before the answer comes. And may thriving, rich faith mark your life in every way. You have access to the Most High God. May you live accordingly. Don't give up. Have a great day!

APRIL 11

May you look around and notice all of the answers to prayers you enjoy because of prayers you prayed some time ago, even years ago. May the breakthroughs you've experienced and the open doors you've walked through compel you to pray with more fervency, specificity, and tenacity. God loves your faith. He loves it when you pray. He's very protective of you and won't give you something that's not good for you. He makes you wait because He's making you ready. Keep praying. God is moving, even when you can't see it. One day, your faith will become sight.

APRIL 12

Perhaps your world has been rocked today by devastating news. Or maybe you are dealing with what others might consider seemingly insignificant issues. I'm reminded of a story Beth Moore shared several years ago. She was sitting in a Bible Study and prayer requests were being shared. She had something she was dealing with at the time and was about to share when the lady sitting next to her announced she had just been diagnosed with cancer. Beth thought to herself, I cannot ask for prayer for my small issue when this dear lady has just received this news. Beth went on to share that at the moment God spoke to her heart. "Beth, from the irritations to the devastations, bring them to Me." No matter how insignificant your problem appears, it is important to Him. He cares for you. He loves you. Whatever it is you're facing, He is here. He is our security, our fortress, our hope, our comfort and our answer. Never feel like it isn't important enough to take to Him, He wants us to turn to Him.

APRIL 13

How do we thrive in the middle of the chaos of this world, in the middle of heartache, in the middle of health crises? The enemy of your soul has one purpose, to take away-steal-kill-destroy. The enemy is a scumbag to put it more bluntly. But...God. We have a God who is faithful, trustworthy, and reliable. A God who will bring healing to the hurting, peace to the hearts, comfort during crises and tragedies. He will never forsake us. He will never leave us. He is always with us even when we can't "feel" Him. He is real. So, when doubts come roaring like a flood, when despair settles in, when loneliness is prevalent... He is our doubt slayer, He is our despair warrior, and He is our best friend.

APRIL 14

I heard a lot of references to the phrase "new normal" during the pandemic. Life will never return to the same as it was before a loss of a loved one, loss of a loved career, loss of a friendship, and this awful pandemic of the past few years. As you walk through your everyday life, that has become the temporary or even permanent "new normal," scoot a little closer to Jesus, lean in, and listen to what He has to say to you. He loves you. He cherishes you. He has hopes for you. He wants to heal you, restore you, and renew you. His truth will set you free. His power will part the waters. His love will heal your soul. His heart for you will make you whole. Lean in, listen for His voice—His gentle, powerful, redemptive, and life-giving voice. Dare to believe who you can be because of Him. Miracles still happen in the middle of chaos, tragedy and storms. Have a blessed and beautiful day!

APRIL 15

May God lift you up and heal and restore you fully. May you see glimpses of His glory everywhere you turn. May He show you wonders of His love that overwhelm you and make your knees weak. May He put a new song in your heart and a new dream in your spirit. May you walk forward unafraid and full of faith that your future will be far greater than your past. Embrace a faith-filled perspective this weekend. May you be keenly aware, you're only passing through. God is not finished with your story yet.

Believe when you pray: Father in heaven, I lift my soul to You and ask you to revive me once again. Bring truth to the deepest places of my soul, where insecurities go to hide. Fill me fresh with the knowledge of You and Your love. Remind me again how to think like an heir. Help me to walk worthy of Your name. Lord, my heart longs to see a breakthrough, but I will praise You in the meantime. You are good, Your promises are true, and You will make a way for me. I entrust my cares to You, and I rejoice resting in Your embrace, because I know You've got me and You're working in ways I can't see. May I wake up each morning ready and revived, purposeful and passionate, and anointed and appointed to face the day. Thank You for loving me like You do. Thank you for sending your Son for a world that is still full of the ungrateful. Amen.

APRIL 16

May Jesus increase His territory through you! Allow Him more access to your soul, more influence in your life, and more voice in your choices. When you come to the edges of yourself and you're hemmed in by your own humanity, don't despair, rejoice! There's more of Jesus for you! The enemy of your soul wants you to focus on your disappointments and limitations. The Savior of your soul wants you to look up, trust Him, and believe Him for great things. Don't let your heart be troubled. May Jesus answer your prayers and profoundly love the world through you.

APRIL 17

I've seen a lot of social media posts supporting this one and condemning that one. Everyone has their own personal and sometimes collective opinion. What I choose to read, from The Word, and believe is HIS opinion. May God's opinion matter far more to you than man's opinion. May His dreams for you speak louder than your fears. May you refuse to read into situations that make you anxious. May Jesus's promise to protect and provide be enough for you. His forgiveness washes over every sin from your past. You can rise up in the knowledge that He's made you brand new, through and through. No spot or stain on you. Walk free today. Show compassion today. Speak with kindness today. Be a friend today. Be the one who others can trust.

APRIL 18

God's will and plan aren't the way we think they should be. Neither does He reveal it all at once. Step by step, day by day. What is His plan for your life? What is His plan for your future? Maybe the better question is, am I offering my life, fully, to God? Once we offer our lives to Him, without reservation...then we will be able to begin seeing His plans laid out for our lives. Sometimes when He asks us to do something, it can seem insane. When He placed words in your heart to write, don't be afraid to publish that book. When he opens a different door than the career you've been in for years, don't be afraid to walk through that door. When He tells you to prepare, like Noah, don't be afraid to be mocked. When He sends you before the Pharaoh, like Moses, don't be afraid to stand for what is right. When He leads, urges, gives you visions or dreams...don't be afraid. There must be an offering before there can be an experience. He will never forsake you when we step in faith.

APRIL 19

May your joy and strength rise with the sun this morning. You have access to these in Christ Jesus. You don't have to wait to feel strong or joyful, you can lay hold of these this minute. Choose to look up this morning, before you take another step. Remind your soul that you're strong in Him. Encourage your heart that Jesus carries your burdens, and He carries you. He'll do the heavy lifting; you do the trusting. Each day we're faced with countless opportunities to choose faith or fear, determination or despair. Choose life because Jesus is alive in you so on this day, have a blessed day.

APRIL 20

God can give you faith to put fear under your feet. You can know that for every way the enemy comes against you, the Lord has a promise to come through for you and to help you stand strong. Fix your eyes on Jesus, set your face like flint, and set your heart on His word. Know this: when the enemy comes in like a flood, the Lord raises up a standard against him. Trust in God and take your next steps with faith and courage. Have a brave and blessed day.

APRIL 21

May your emotions find rest in God alone while you wait for Him to answer your prayers. Sing a new song even when sighing feels easier to do. Smile even through the tears. Be assured, when things look their worst, God is working His best for you. Slow down and sit down for a while, just for rest and reflection. Keep climbing, even when the climb feels impossible and the goal unobtainable. God is guiding your steps and your efforts will be rewarded. It's okay to fail and to fall, that's when we learn Who is the One to pick us up. When you get up again, you will find new resolve to stand firmly on God's promises and you can walk forward in faith. Let us realize when we feel like it's easier laying on our backs, it's actually more beneficial falling to our knees. If you take one humble, bold step at a time, you'll eventually put your toes on your promised land. Keep climbing, always looking up and never looking down. We have better times ahead of us than behind. Jesus goes before you. He's got your back, just keep climbing. And He's placed His hand of blessing on your head (Ps. 139:5). Have a monumental and awesome day!

APRIL 22

May God lift your chin, awaken your heart, and open your eyes to all you possess in Him. Refuse to let your disappointments define you. When standing on what you think is barren land, envision a harvest. Experience a revival of faith in that very place that once appeared barren and empty. Instead of reflecting and rehashing your losses, determine to rehearse His promises because they're truer than your circumstances. Today's a good day to embrace faith, to give thanks, and to worship the One who keeps His promises. Jesus loves you and He is faithful to His word. His love defines you and His promises embrace you and solidify your hope. You've got everything you need in Him. Have a blessed day.

APRIL 23

May you believe that your wildest God-given dreams can come true. Trust Jesus enough to follow Him through the valley to lay hold of them. Be patient and purposeful. Allow your selfish ambition to die and your holy ambition to arise. Lean into your training time so you'll be prepared and strengthened to stand in your next place of promise. Then you'll be poised to change the world. God loves to work mightily through His children, and He intends to use you. May you have startling clarity and abounding faith in the days ahead. Rest in Him today and follow His lead, every single step of the way. Blessings are yours on this day!

APRIL 24

We are in this together yet, we are in different places, experiencing different fears and concerns. One thing will always remain the same, God is still in control, and He is in this with us. We are not alone, even when it feels that way. He is with us in the fire. He is with us in the storm. He is with us in this pandemic. He will always be with us and never will forsake us. God's assurance is He loves you. Be blessed today, no matter where you are in uncertainty, because He has you.

APRIL 25

Have you ever been swimming in the ocean, lake, or river and fought to keep your head above water and strength to keep going because the current was so strong? Have you ever tried to walk through a bad wind, and it took all your strength to keep standing upright? We can look at it from a spiritual perspective. The world, culture, the enemy of our soul comes against us over and over and we feel we are constantly struggling, even fighting, against the current. The winds of despair blow and we feel like we can't stand. Oh, but GOD...He gives us the strength to stand and move against the current when He is the center of our lives. Faith is under attack. Marriage is under attack. Families are under attack. Be wise, know who God is. Develop a firm foundation of a relationship with Him. He is our strength, He makes us more than an overcomer, He is our sustainable source. Stand firm on this day.

APRIL 26

May God lift your chin, awaken your heart, and open your eyes to all you possess in Him. Refuse to let your disappointments define you. Experience a revival of faith in that very place. Instead of rehashing your losses, determine to rehearse His promises because they're truer than your circumstances. Today's a good day to embrace faith, to give thanks, and to worship the One who keeps His promises. Jesus loves you and He is faithful to His word. His love defines you and His promises hem you in and shore you up. You've got everything you need in Him. Have faith full day!

APRIL 27

May you sense God's invitation to believe Him for something more, something greater, something deeper. He's always on the move and He invites you to move with Him. As He shows you areas of your life where you struggle with unbelief, may you refuse despair, and instead respond in prayer: "Lord, awaken fresh faith in me!" He holds out His hand and bids you to walk on the water with Him, to trust

Him for what breaks your heart, and to believe that some of those dreams in your heart were put there by Him. Look up and trust Him today. He is faithful to His word and He's made specific promises to you.

APRIL 28

May God Himself release fresh faith and perspective into your soul today! He strengthens your resolve and establishes your steps. He surrounds you with good friends who fear God and who love you. He will give you fresh vision for your future and divine wisdom for stewarding your "now" moments. Allow the song in your heart to ring louder than the enemy's threats and accusations. There is no one like our God and there's nothing like His love for you! Walk blessed today because you are!

APRIL 29

Have you ever felt you're just going through the motions? In life? At work? At home? When with family or friends? If we are truthful, we all have at some point in our lives. Maybe even more often than not, we are on autopilot. Refuse the auto-pilot life. Instead, be a lean-in-and-listen kind of person. Be quick to discern the Lord's whisper and be quick to follow His lead. Notice the winds of change blowing in the trees and loosen your tent stakes if the Lord requires it. Cup your ear toward heaven and treasure the Lord's voice above all others. Enjoy your day today!

APRIL 30

May the Lord Himself lift you up and make you strong. He fills your heart with a song of thanksgiving for ALL He's done and ALL He's about to do! He gives you glimpses of glory, insights into His precious plans for you, enough to put a spring in your step and faith in your heart. God's road ahead of you can take you places you never thought you'd go. May you see answers to prayers, unexpected breakthroughs, and divine outcomes, because you serve our star-breathing God and He's especially taken with you. Have a great day!

DON'T LOSE FOCUS.

DON'T LOSE HOPE.

ALWAYS REMEMBER,

YOUR STORY IS STILL BEING WRITTEN.

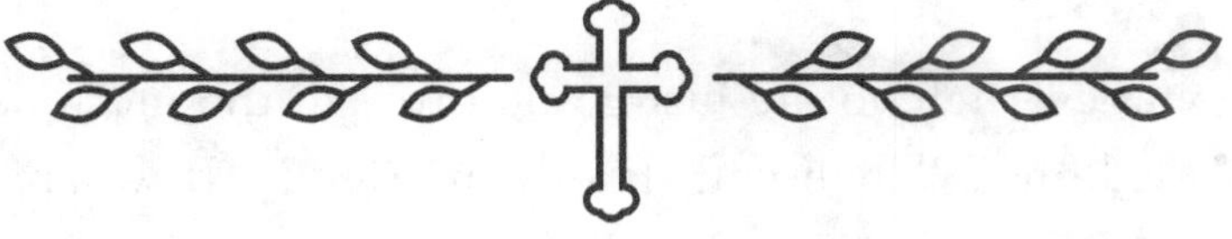

Write Notes:

__/__/__

Write Notes:

__/__/__

May

MAY 1

God is doing a new thing. Can you sense it? Even when it doesn't appear things are changing for your good, they are. Can you hear His voice in the stillness of night or in the quiet moments during the busyness of the day? Lean in and listen to that still small voice and take your next steps with a heart of faith and expectancy. Allow Jesus Himself give you a fresh vision for what breakthrough looks like so you will not lose heart or give up when it seems the battle rages on. Soon, and very soon, you will see and know that His promises are true for you. Strengthen yourself in the Lord today. Remind yourself who you are and whose you are. Recite His promises and rehearse His faithfulness. He's been good and He'll be good, always and forever. Walk forward in faith. God bless you!

MAY 2

We can't know who we are in Christ until we first believe who we are in Christ. When we begin to believe who we are, what we can become in Him. He can begin to restore, renew, and refresh. Only He can give hope. Only He can restore. Only He can make new. Only He can bring unity. Only He can refresh what is fading. He is always faithful. He is always with us, but we must first submit fully to Him. Do you believe who you are in Him? It isn't easy to give Him all of ourselves. Sometimes we hold back a little and we don't even realize it. In the middle of world that seemingly has gone mad, He is a stabilizing force. Let Him secure your foundation today and every day!

MAY 3

May you discern the difference between understanding the times and standing strong in prayer. Stop staring too long at the news and cower in fear. Even though the enemy comes in like a flood, the Lord will raise up a standard against him. Your prayers do matter. God's promises are true. Your perspective is important and matters. Be assured, He moves when you pray. Stand in faith and pray with confidence, because there is a God in heaven who hears you when you pray. Yes, there is a God and He does care and hear you. He is not shaken at fear, nor deaf. He does hear prayers. He see tears flowing like rivers. He cares and He loves you. Though the enemy is on the move, know this: God already has a plan. Stand and be counted. Pray like you mean it. Have a faith-filled, powerful, and prayerful day!

MAY 4

Have you been praying with expectancy? Can you hear the winds of change blowing because of your prayers? Can you feel something different in your heart and spirit? Allow the Lord to enlarge your territory, expand your influence, and increase your capacity to walk in faith. Feel His hand of power be upon you in a way that marks everything you do.

He keeps you from harm—both causing and enduring it. Allow Him to use you to bless a world very much in need. He can surprise you with breakthroughs and still-water Sabbath moments. Walk forward unafraid with the full knowledge that your Shepherd goes before you. He's placed His hand of blessing upon your head, and He will faithfully lead you. Have a lighthearted, joy-filled day today!

MAY 5

May God wildly increase your capacity to walk with Him. May His power and His promises impact your every word and every step. May He increase your territory, establish your influence, and awaken your faith. May He deepen your love, broaden your perspective, and multiply your compassion. In every way, may you know God's redeeming, multiplying power in your life. May humble and holy spiritual momentum be yours. Walk forward in faith today.

MAY 6

Be very careful not to make long-term decisions during short term circumstances! When fatigue and frustration are felt…it is hard to have faith. Hold on…be quick to identify and let go of any lies you pick up along the way today. Shake off any offenses that you're tempted to cling to. May you instead, wrap yourself up in the complete love and affection of Christ. Forgive yourself and forgive others. Believe that God's promises are more powerful than your blunders. Embrace God's redemptive plan for your life with hope and expectancy. You're truly deeply loved. Celebrate today!

MAY 7

May God unearth the unsettled and unhealed places in your life so He can heal, renew, and restore you. Allow Him to reveal a fresh revelation of His love and a new assurance of His grace. Allow Him to pour the oil of joy and gladness over your head. He gives you pools of blessing to splash your feet in. His has unfathomable greatness that can bring a fresh mystery and power to your prayers and perspective. Walk lightly today. He's got you!

MAY 8

May you find shelter beneath the shadow of God's wing. Be wise enough to stay in His established space for you, trusting He'll move you to your next place when the timing is right. His grace empowers you to live abundantly, to stand strong, and to pray powerfully. May your honor for Him compel you to trust Him when your trials seem truer than His word. He will not fail you, will not forget about you, and will not turn away from you. He's with you in battle, He'll help you when your heart breaks, and He'll deliver you and bless you before a watching world when the time is right. Trust Him. Know that you're so very dear to His heart.

MAY 9

May the Lord establish in you a healthy, divine rhythm of life. He strengthens you in mind, body, and spirit. Where you're broken, He restores, where you're weary, He refreshes where you're fearful, He revives faith. May your intimate walk with Jesus trump everything else in your life. Let your heart for Him inspire every choice you make. Speak your prayers and take on a new conviction because you know Jesus better today than you did yesterday. Walk in humble, bold faith today. God's promises are truer than you know and He's kinder than you can fathom. Blessings to you on this day!

MAY 10

May you pause today, look back over your shoulder, and remember the ways God has been good to you, has come through for you, and has kept His word to you. Look ahead in faith with expectancy, as you get a sense of the land. He wants you to claim. Feel your faith rise up within you as you take your first steps in that direction. Embrace a renewed resolve to walk intimately with the One who loves you and has a beautiful plan for your life. He deserves some sacred space in your day today! Blessings to you, my friend!

MAY 11

May God grant you abundant grace and a right perspective. He instills in your heart and mind new courage to stand strong and think long. When you are amidst hardships—remember who you are. Move forward from this place, pray powerful prayers based on God's goodness and feel your connection to Him. You're His. He is yours. Dare to stand in faith and hang on until the storm passes. Soon the sun will break through the clouds and Jesus will bring clarity to your soul. Until then, trust God and remember that He is good even when life is hard.

May 12

Have you ever felt stretched so thin because you were trying to do too much? Help too many people? Involved in too many projects? Has the guilt of saying "NO" felt overwhelming? It's okay to say no. It's okay to stop and take time for yourself. Be content to know that you cannot be all things to all people; you live to serve an audience of One. You can love people but keep your hope in God. Be willing to take risks with people but put your sole trust in God. Allow the power you once gave to others rest solely on God because He defines, He saves, He provides, and He has the power to transform. You have nothing to prove and all of eternity to live for. Walk free today because you can! Blessings on your day today!

May 13

Have you ever known someone who believed in you, someone who frequently spoke words of encouragement and praise? The kind of person who made you feel you could do it, whatever the "it" was? That's the kind of person God wants us to be. Have you ever said, "God is all I need?" He is. He placed others in our lives because we need each other. We need each other for companionship, friendship, and emotional support. Social connection can lower anxiety and depression, help us regulate our emotions, lead to higher self-esteem and empathy, and actually improve our immune systems. Challenge yourself to be an encouragement to someone today. When we help others, it gives us a sense of satisfaction and freedom. Don't worry what others think, you were created to be You! You are accepted, you are secure, and you are free! Accept this for yourself and speak it to someone else today. Christ has made us free.

MAY 14

(Speak this one over yourself): I am deeply loved, divinely appointed, abundantly equipped, and profoundly cherished by God. No enemy plan, scheme, or obstacle can keep me from God's highest and best will for me. As I follow the voice of my Savior, I see the invisible, accomplish the impossible, and love the unlovable. I am a living-breathing miracle because Jesus Christ lives in me! I refuse insecurity and wrap my arms around bold conviction and humble faith because Jesus has offered these to me! In His precious Name I stand, live, and pray. Amen.

MAY 15

Look around and notice all of the answers to prayers that you enjoy because of those prayers you prayed some time ago. Breakthroughs you've experienced and the opened doors you've walked through because of your prayers can compel you to pray with more fervency, specificity, and tenacity. God loves your faith. He loves your heart. He loves it when you pray. He's very protective of you and won't give you something that's not good for you. He makes you wait because He's making you ready. Trust with your whole soul and story to Him. And keep praying. God is moving, even when you can't see it. One day, your faith will become sight. A blessed, beautiful, and prayerful day to you today!

MAY 16

The question is do you love Him, do you put your trust and faith in Him, do you identify with being a Christ follower? We should live our lives that parallels to The Word. Loving Him, trusting in Him and following Him doesn't mean we will never fall, we will never fail, we will never falter, we will never stumble or have doubts. What loving Him and trusting Him means is we are victorious and overcomers. When we fall and fail, we get up and start again. I've done this many times during my life. If we are honest, we've all had times of failure, we all have stumbled, we all have doubts. But...God gives us the ability to get up, dust ourselves off and look to Him to begin again. Life is hard, but His love is secure. When the unexpected phone call announcing heartbreak, the loss of a long-time career, a discouraging medical report, feelings of isolation and anxiety comes, God is our source of encouragement and strength. I encourage you to look to Him. Have encouragement and peace today!

MAY 17

Pause today and listen for God's gentle whisper in your ear. Respond to the slightest nudge of the Spirit within you and do the next thing God gives you to do. Refuse to get your perspective from the surface appearance of things. Lean in and look for The Lord in this place. He has something for you here; something you need to take with you to your next place of promise. Remember that in every single step of the way, you are His. He's got you. Have a wise, discerning day today.

MAY 18

May you embrace the grace to leave your past in God's hands. Have the grit to face down your fears. Have the gumption to go after your God-given dreams. See God's glory shining over every part of your life. Jesus gives good gifts to His children. Put the lies under your feet and embrace God's truth deep within your heart. You're on a pilgrimage to a most holy place. Keep walking. Keep believing. "Yes You, LORD, are our Father. We are the clay; you are the potter; we are all the work of your hand." Isaiah 64:8 (New International Version)

MAY 19

May you believe that your wildest God-given dreams can come true. Trust Jesus enough to follow Him through the valley to lay hold of them. Be patient and purposeful. Allow your selfish ambition to die and your holy ambition to arise. Lean into your training time so you'll be prepared and strengthened to stand in your next place of promise. Then you'll be poised to change the world. God loves to work mightily through His children, and He intends to use you. You can have startling clarity and abounding faith in the days ahead. Rest in Him today and follow His lead, every single step of the way. Blessings on your day.

MAY 20

May God wildly increase your capacity to walk with Him. Seek His power and His promises to impact your every word and every step. Allow Him to increase your territory, establish your influence, and awaken your faith. Feel Him deepen your love, broaden your perspective, and multiply your compassion. In every way, you can know God's redeeming, multiplying power in your life. May humble and holy spiritual momentum be yours. Walk forward in faith today.

MAY 21

May God unearth the unsettled and unhealed places in your life so He can heal, renew, and restore you. Let Him reveal a fresh revelation of His love and a new assurance of His grace. Allow Him to pour the oil of joy and gladness over your head. He gives you pools of blessing to splash your feet in. May His unfathomable greatness bring a fresh mystery and power to your prayers and perspective. Today is for healing from His greatness.

MAY 22

As this day draws to a close, embrace God's grace, trusting He'll fill every gap. Instead of being unsettled by your imperfections, open your heart and feel Jesus's perfect love for you. Instead of fretting over your missteps, rejoice that He never left your side today. Scoop this day into your hand and lift it up as an offering to the One who moves mountains and administers miracles with every little handful, we give Him. He's a miracle working God and He loves you. Close today with a joyful heart.

MAY 23

In your days ahead, take your cues from God (and not from culture), and become a powerful, praying warrior! Dream big dreams with God! Pray prayers that make your knees buckle and your heart tremble as you entrust your whole soul and story to the God of the Universe. He intends to solve some of the world's problems through you. When the enemy comes in like a flood, the Lord raises a standard against him. This is no time for cowering in fear. This is your time to rise up in faith! Trust God's Word. Believe His promises. Do what He says. And in due time, you'll see the waters part, the mountains move, and the answers you've been waiting for. You are mighty in God. Walk full-of-faith today!

MAY 24

May the veil between heaven and earth seem especially thin. Sense, like never before, the presence and the power of the living God. Jesus won the victory. He defeated death and sin. He made a public spectacle of the powers that oppose us. Though you have troubles and trials, you serve a strong and mighty God who means what He says and does what He says He'll do. One day there'll be no more tears; no more war; no more hatred. Keep walking. Keep believing because you're only passing through. You're heaven bound. Live like it's true today and have a most blessed day!

MAY 25

When you're weary and tired, may God give you rest and a right perspective. When you long to run ahead on your own, allow Him to give you divine wisdom to wait on Him. When the road seems long and never ending, remember He is with you during the entire journey. He is faithful. It is His business to take care of us, fulfill His promises, and our business to believe His word and Promises are true. When your guard is down and you're vulnerable to the enemy's schemes, seek God's protection and He will deliver you on every side. When you're ready to fly, He lifts you up and blesses you before a watching world. Take one humble step at a time. He'll lead you to your next place of promise. May deep nourishing, refreshing faith be yours today.

MAY 26

God has eyes on you, and He is the Most High God. You have not been forgotten and you will surely rise to your destiny, for this time and place. You've been patient and waited, now watch Him move on your behalf. You have been crying out and He has heard and bottled those tears. May we realize our worth and potential. Realize you are about to give birth to a new thing. Feel His presence of healing today!

MAY 27

God is doing a new thing with you and in your life. Can you sense it? Lean in and listen to that still small voice and take your next steps with a heart of faith and expectancy. Jesus Himself gives you a fresh vision for what breakthrough looks like so you will not lose heart or give up when it seems the battle rages on. Soon, and very soon, you will see and know that His promises are true for you. Strengthen yourself in the Lord today. Remind yourself who you are and whose you are. Recite His promises and rehearse His faithfulness. He's been good and He'll be good, always and forever. Walk forward in faith today!

MAY 28

May your deep desire for God's presence and power eclipse every lesser thing in your life. Let your hunger for His holiness make you lose your taste for toxic time wasters. Allow your desire to see Him move mightily compel you to move outside your comfort zone and obey Him even when it doesn't suit you. His passion for you ignites your passion for Him. Nothing–absolutely nothing compares to knowing the Lord of Angel Armies. Here's what's true: He delights in you. Allow your whole life to reflect His glory today and every day.

May 29

Seek to have this season be one of Rest, Revival, and Renewal. Experience the REST of God in your most trying circumstances; and as a result, find peace and bear fruit where's there's only been anxiety, fear and troublesome-prickly-thorns. Experience a personal REVIVAL that changes how you pray, what you say, and where you put your time. Experience such soul RENEWAL that even the old things in your life feel new. God doesn't make things "nice." He makes things "new." Trust Him to do a brand-new work in you in the days ahead.

May 30

May God answer your accumulative prayers for those you love. Let Him draw near them by His Spirit. He can heal their deepest wounds, restore their perspective, make their crooked ways straight, and open their eyes where they're blind. God Himself drives a wedge between every person and circumstance that the enemy is using to lie to and distract your loved ones from God's best for them. He lines their path with people and circumstances that speak life-giving, soul-restoring truth until they're totally free! Seek a revival break out, see the prodigals come home, feel the weary be restored, and the broken healed. Wait together for God to do what only He can do. He moves when we pray. Rest in the promise that God loves your loved one far more passionately than you do! Choose Joy in the meantime.

May 31

May the Lord enlarge your territory, expand your influence, and increase your capacity to walk in faith. Feel His hand of power upon you in a way that marks everything you do. He keeps you from harm—both causing and enduring it—and He uses you to bless a world very much in need. Allow Him to surprise you with breakthroughs and still-water-refreshing moments. Walk forward unafraid with the full knowledge that Your Shepherd goes before you. He's placed His hand of blessing upon your head, and He will faithfully lead you. Have a lighthearted, joy-filled day today!

Don't lose focus.

Don't lose hope.

Always remember,

your story is still being written.

Write Notes:

__/__/__

Write Notes:

__/__/__

June

JUNE 1

Enjoy life and your day. I just want to encourage you to make time for those you love—family and friends. Make time to sit and watch a sunrise and a sunset. Rebuke and refuse thoughts that weaken, discourage, or pull you down and always remember how deeply and profoundly God loves you and someone loves and needs you on this earth. If you live out of the love of God, you'll be a wellspring of life for others. Always be assured and remember—you are a treasured creation. May you embrace every sacred and precious moment God gives you and give it back as an offering of praise. Speak a kind and encouraging word! Keeping in mind...our footsteps are ordered! Life on earth is short. Eternity is long. Live with eternity in mind. God's richest blessings to you and those you love.

JUNE 2

In the days ahead, may you die to the power of others' opinions that you may live out of the relentless, abundant love God has for you. As people become crueler and more careless with their opinions, and even actions, may you become more loving and discerning with yours. May you speak with compassion, pray with power, and stand in courage. Your life and influence matter deeply in this desperate world. Lean in and learn everything you can from the One who loves you deeply and intends to use you greatly. A blessed and beautiful day to you on this day!

June 3

God is doing a new thing. Can you sense it? May you lean in and listen to that still small voice and take your next steps with a heart of faith and expectancy. Allow Jesus Himself give you a fresh vision for what breakthrough looks like so you will not lose heart or give up when it seems the battle rages on. Soon, and very soon, you will see and know that His promises are true for you. Strengthen yourself in the Lord today. Remind yourself who you are and whose you are. Recite His promises and rehearse His faithfulness. He's been good and He'll be good, always and forever. Walk forward in faith. God bless you!

June 4

May this next season for you be one of Rest, Revival, and Renewal. Experience the REST of God in your most trying circumstances; and as a result, find peace and bear fruit where's there's only been anxiety, fear and troublesome-prickly-thorns. Experience a personal REVIVAL that changes how you pray, what you say, and where you put your time. May you experience such soul RENEWAL that even the old things in your life feel new. God doesn't make things "nice." He makes things "new." Trust Him to do a brand-new work in you in the days ahead, starting with today!

JUNE 5

May you entrust your whole soul and story to the God who saves, loves, and establishes you. May you come to know, more and more, that He leads you even when you're unaware. The less you lean on your own understanding (and trust in His direction instead), the more you'll enjoy the peace that passes understanding and defies your circumstance. God is with you. He is for you. And He will never, no never, forsake you. Open your hands, receive the love He gladly gives, and walk with a spring in your step today. His mercy covers you and His grace surrounds you. Have a joyful day on this day!

JUNE 6

May you determine to be done with captivity! No more rehearsing your failures or rehashing your critics' accusations. It's time to remember God's love, His faithfulness, and His heart of affection for you. It's time to put all of your hope in the finished work of Jesus Christ. Put a flag in the ground this day and declare, "My hope is built on nothing less but Jesus's blood and righteousness!" Rest in God's grace. Rely on His love. And rehearse His promises because they're true for you. Break free from the bondage of others' opinions and walk free and full of faith this day!

JUNE 7

May you be highly discerning in the days ahead! Recognize when God is asking you to solidify your faith and stand strong, and when He's inviting you hide yourself under the shadow of His wing. May you quickly discern the enemy's schemes and stay clear of the traps he sets for you. In spite of your mistakes, missteps, and misunderstandings, may you never doubt your worth and your value. You're someone God loves, treasures, anoints, and appoints. He'll show Himself strong in your weakness, faithful in your fears, and merciful where you fall short. Walk wisely with Him today and be aware that your footsteps are ordered by The Lord. There's a best place, a best path for your feet. Don't let fear keep your feet planted in one place when He is opening new paths. Take every step with Jesus in the days to come, with faith and peace. Have a wise, discerning day.

June 8

As the winds of change start to blow in your life, lean in and listen for the voice of the Lord. Instead of looking for "signs" and mistakenly drawing the wrong conclusion, may you instead look to the Lord and His strength. He'll speak to you in a way you'll understand. He'll lead you in the way you should go. He is faithful and true and He's doing a NEW thing in your life! Keep your ear bent toward heaven. Daily the heavens pour forth speech. May you listen for every word today and every day!

June 9

May God give you perspective on the things that frustrate you. May your heart of compassion grow for those who suffer in unimaginable ways. May you pray as passionately for them as you do for yourself. May God protect you from a small, selfish mindset. May He fill you up with thanksgiving and joy for the freedoms you enjoy! May He renew your resolve to be a grateful, humble soul. And may He use you today in ways that surprise and bless you. Don't lose focus. Don't lose hope. Always remember, your story is still being written!

JUNE 10

May God release special favor over your life today! Allow Him to fill you up to overflowing and give you a fresh vision for your life. Identify the places where the enemy has planted inferiority and insecurity and play king of the hill there! Put him under your feet, refuse to let those lies win the day. In Christ you have NO reason to feel less than or inferior. He is more than enough for you. Walk in God's truth and rest in His care. He loves you and He'll lead you in the way you should go. Have a blessed day today!

JUNE 11

May you be so sensitive to God's voice that you rest when He says rest and run when He says run. He knows what's best for you and He'll get you where you need to go. When it comes to your pace and your choices, people will always have their opinions about you, but God offers His power to you. He's the One who knows your frame, your steps, and your STORY. Trust Him and do what He says. Though there are giants in the land, you have God on your side. Be brave. Be strong. Be courageous. He's got you.

JUNE 12

May the hilarious joy of the Lord be your strength today! May a fresh awakening of faith sturdy your steps. Allow a new song in your heart remind you that God has been good to you, and He'll be good again. Raise your hands in praise because you are prized, loved, accepted, called, equipped, and sent to reach a world in need. Delight in God today. He will establish you. Rejoice in Him. He will strengthen you.

Trust in Him. He will not fail you. Give your burdens to Him and wrap yourself up in His grace. You have what you need to abound in every good work. He's got you covered. A blessed and joy-full day to you.

JUNE 13

He is the way that will see you through suffering...His word has been proven tried and true. His word is truth, that will never lead us astray...His word will make a way when there seems to be no way. He is the life...He gives us hope in the middle of suffering. He transforms our lives. Cultivate a lifestyle that creates space for grace, growth, and transformation. A complete metamorphosis of every part of your life. Guard against toxic thoughts, attitudes, and mindsets that only weaken you. Instead, fill your thoughts with all that's lovely, praiseworthy, and truthful. In the days ahead, may your intimate walk with Jesus form your decisions, renew your prayers, and exemplify your love. Guard your thoughts, focus, and hide His words in your heart and it'll change your life. We are on an ongoing transformation...always progressing. The struggle is the point of suffering, and it will bring you through victorious.

JUNE 14

May you discern the difference between understanding the times and standing strong in prayer and staring too long at the news and cowering in fear. Though the enemy comes in like a flood, the Lord WILL raise up a standard against him. Your prayers matter. God's promises are true. Your perspective matters. And He moves when you pray. Stand in faith, pray like there's a God in heaven who hears you when you pray, because He does! Though the enemy is on the move, know this: God already has a plan. Stand in faith and pray like you mean it. Have a faith-filled, powerful, and prayerful day.

June 15

May you dare to believe that God is moving in your life because He is. He makes all things new. And He intends to dismantle the schemes of the enemy. Will you trust Him? Make your next steps as faith-steps and make your next words as faith-words. Embrace a joyful heart, not because of what your eyes see, but because of what your heart knows: God is good, He is for you, and He will not fail you. Have a blessed day.

June 16

May you trade your energy zappers for things that nourish your soul, renew your spirit and strength. Turn your back on influences that diminish your identity and distract you from Jesus Christ. Be brave enough to discard emotional leeches. Give more time to words, thoughts, and songs that remind you who you are in Him. Carefully guard your tastes and preferences so you don't lose your appetite for the things of God. Nothing on this earth and no one else can satisfy our souls' deepest longings like Jesus can. You are made for Him. You were created for a purpose. Your life has substance and meaning. Your journey is no accident. Your footsteps have been ordered and set in motion. Seek to find your hope, peace, purpose and life in Him today!

June 17

May God unearth the unsettled and unhealed places in your life so He can heal, renew, and restore you. He will reveal a fresh revelation of

His love and a new assurance of His grace. Accept his pouring the oil of joy and gladness over your head. Seek His pools of blessing splashed to your feet. Accept His unfathomable greatness bring a fresh mystery and power to your prayers and perspective. Walk confidently in the assurance of His unwavering love on this day and every day.

June 18

May you look around and notice all of the answers to prayers and enjoy because of prayers you prayed were some time ago. Experience the past open doors you've walked through and allow them to compel you to pray with more fervency, specificity, and tenacity. God loves your faith. He loves your heart. He loves it when you pray. He's very protective of you and won't give you something that's not good for you. He makes you wait because He's making you ready. Trust your whole soul and story to Him. And keep praying. God is moving, even when you can't see it. One day, your faith will become sight. A blessed, beautiful, and prayerful day to you.

June 19

Let this be our prayer today: Precious Lord, forgive me for my tendency to worry and be anxious! I embrace Your grace for the race today. I will turn my back on worry and turn my face toward Your promises! You are all that I need. Help me to rest in the shadow of Your wing where no enemy can reach me. Help me to run the race with the strength You provide. And help me to refuse thoughts that pull me out of that place of peace. May my mind, body, and spirit thrive as I stay in the center of Your will for me today. Amen.

June 20

When your faith-seeds are in the ground and the harvest is yet to come, may you use the time in between to care for your soul and to know Jesus more. Are you weary? Give priority to rest. Are you disillusioned? Take some time in God's presence and let Him renew your perspective. Do you feel beat up by life? Draw near to Jesus so He can restore you. Even when the sky is dark and blackness appears to surround, He is beside you. Don't forget who you are in this season of life. You're loved, treasured, called, and appointed. God has not lost your address. He knows where you live. And at just the right time, He will break through. Embrace faith and courage!

June 21

When life knocks you down, may you get back up again because God is mighty in you! When your rogue emotions turn you upside down, may you find your footing again because your rock is Christ. When the clouds block the sun and your perspective dims, may God Himself break through with a fresh reminder of His promises. May the changeable things in your life take a back seat to the unchangeable, never-ending love and faithfulness of God. He has given you a solid place to stand. Don't lose focus. Don't lose hope. Always remember, your story is still being written.

June 22

When you feel like you don't fit in, may you walk in faith because you have a place at the Table of Grace. When you feel like you're just not enough, may you remember that His enough is more than enough for you. When you trip up and fall short, remember that He stoops down to make you great. And when you don't feel victorious, remember that you're already seated with Christ because He won the victory for you.

JUNE 23

May you pause today and reflect on the wonder of what it means to have Christ living in you! May His peace abide in you and restore your soul. May His healing come alive in you and make you whole. May His strength rise up in you and make you strong! And may His love overwhelm you and fill your heart with a new song! His life in yours changes everything. He's holding you and promises to never let you go. When your arms get tired, rest in His, because it's His strong arms that will sustain you. He loves you, He's in you, so you have all you need. Rejoice in the wonderful reality of Christ in you! A beautiful day is yours on this day!

JUNE 24

As you step back and survey the parts of your life that break your heart or that don't make sense right now, may you dare to stand strong, look up, and consider afresh what God's resurrection POWER can do in, though, and around you! Only those who've walked through the valley of the shadow will truly grasp the power of redemption on the other side. Jesus withholds NO good thing from those who walk intimately with Him. He's not the reason you suffer; He's with you in the storm. He is your Shelter, Deliverer, and Strong Tower. He's Your Redeemer, Savior, and Friend. He's your Prince of Peace and Sure Defender. Find your footing again. Engage your faith. Embrace the right perspective. Trust Jesus with your whole heart and see what Love will do.

June 25

May the phrase "let go and let God" take on a whole new meaning for you. Learn to rest while He works on your behalf. Try to understand your role in this Kingdom story and do only what He tells you to do. Trust Him in the process. Live free from the bondage of others' opinions so you're free to love them the way Christ does. Allow others to be so drawn to your healed heart that they come to know Jesus for themselves. Unclench your fists, untangle your fears, and entrust your heart and story to the One who loves you deeply and cares for you profoundly. Let Him work while you trust. He's really good at what He does. Have a light-hearted day today and make a conscious effort to be kind.

June 26

Enjoy life and your day. I just want to encourage you to make time for those you love—family and friends. Make time to sit and watch a sunrise and a sunset. Rebuke and refuse thoughts that weaken, discourage, or pull you down and always remember how deeply and profoundly God loves you and someone loves and needs you on this earth. If you live out of the love of God, you'll be a wellspring of life for others. Always be assured and remember—You are a treasured creation. Embrace every sacred and precious moment God gives you and give it back as an offering of praise. Speak a kind and encouraging word! Keeping in mind...our footsteps are ordered! Life on earth is short. Eternity is long. Live with eternity in mind. God's richest blessings to you and those you love!

JUNE 27

May God surprise you today with oasis moments of refreshment and encouragement. Allow Him to delight your heart with a kind and unexpected word. He can use you as a source of refreshment to many. Pause today, notice the good things about your day, look up and give thanks. You are blessed and loved, and you have access to a divine supply you could never exhaust or use up. Be present in the moment and trust God to give you what you need today. Blessings on your day!

JUNE 28

May you be diligent about taking time to pause and reflect on the many ways God has blessed you. May you cultivate a heart that knows how to rest in God alone. Though storms rage all around us, we know the One who calms the storm. Take every chance you get to spend time with God, think about His love, and trust His direction in your life. As you look to Him, your whole countenance will change, and others will be reminded that there's a God in heaven very much involved in our lives. He intends to get us safely home. But don't wait 'till then to find rest in Him. Embrace a joyful, faith-filled, hope-full, love-filled day today!

JUNE 29

May God's opinion matter far more to you than man's opinion. His desires for you speak louder than your fears. Refuse to read into situations that make you anxious. Know that Jesus's promise to protect and provide are sufficient for you. His forgiveness washes over every sin from your past. Rise up in the knowledge that He's made you brand new, through and through. No spot or stain on you! Walk in His love today!

June 30

May God revive the areas of your life where you've lost hope and expectancy. Grow to believe on a whole new level and know that Jesus makes all things new! He can make something out of nothing! Look up right now and dare to believe again. God is on His throne. Jesus prays for you. And the Holy Spirit moves on faith. Don't let go of hope. Believe that God redeems. Rest in the reality of God's awesome love, power, and faithfulness. He'll do for you what you cannot do for yourself. Blessings today!

Don't lose focus.

Don't lose hope.

Always remember,

your story is still being written.

Write Notes:

__/__/__

July

JULY 1

Enjoy life and your day! Make time for those you love—family and friends. Take time to sit and watch the sunrise and sunset. Rebuke and refuse thoughts that weaken, discourage, or pull you down. Always remember how deeply and profoundly God loves you and someone loves and needs you on this earth. If you live out of the love of God, you'll be a wellspring of life for others. Be assured and remember—you are a treasured creation. Embrace every sacred and precious moment God gives you and give it back as an offering of praise. Speak a kind and encouraging word. Keep in mind...our footsteps are ordered. Life on earth is short. Eternity is long. Live with eternity in mind. This day experience God's richest blessings to you and those you love.

JULY 2

May God surround you with a strong sense of His great love for you! Live every day with the expectancy that He is moving in your life. Allow the Word of God come alive to you in a way you've never experienced. Feel your prayers take on a whole new level of power and faith. You are His child, and He is with you every step of the way. Blessings to you.

July 3

May you dare to keep walking even though quitting feels like the easier thing to do. Dare to look up even though the weight of your burden compels you to look down. Dare to dream about the future even though the enemy would love for your past to have the last say. Keep walking, looking up, and dare to dream. Jesus invites you forward, taking one step at a time. May God Himself restore to you something you lost and never thought you'd get back again. Feel Him heal a soul wound you thought you'd never get over. Allow Him to pour out an abundance of joy and hope that makes you celebrate before the answer comes. Enjoy a thriving and rich faith marking your life in every way. You have access to the Most High God. Live accordingly.

July 4

May you find a new freedom in being the YOU God created you to be. Be comfortable in your own skin, excited about your own story, and at peace with your own past because Christ has redeemed every part of you. Freedom always comes at a price, as our founding fathers sacrificed all they had to give birth to a new nation. Years before our nation was even a thought, Christ gave His life to give us a new birth. You can break free from condemnation and walk away from toxic influences and put your fear under your feet. Let faith fill your heart. Do not give people the power that belongs to God alone. He loves you. He is strong. And He'll keep you strong 'till the end. It is not coincidental that the National Bird for America is the eagle. We will rise on eagles' wings. We are strong, courageous, and powerful together.

"...but they who wait for the Lord shall renew their strength; they shall mount up with wings like eagles; they shall run and not be weary; they shall walk and not faint." (Isaiah 40:31 KJV)

Have a faith-filled Independence Day!

July 5

God has a destiny for you. He has a place for you and a purpose that He wants you to live out. But it may not happen tomorrow. You probably won't get there by going in a straight line. Rarely does God take someone to the destiny He has for them without taking them on a detour...or two or 10 or even 100. Detours are for a greater purpose. They will make us stronger, more determined, and resilient. It is the one-in-a-million Christian who gets to go from point A to B to C and straight on to Z. Most often, God takes us from A to F to D to R to B to Q and so on. We never know which letter He's pulling out next, either. That's why patience is a preeminent virtue needed in order to reach our destiny.

Detours can disappoint, but delay does not mean denial. We must allow detours to produce hope. God promises that hope will not disappoint

July 6

May peace flow like a river through the very depths of your being. May joy rise within you like the morning sun. Allow strength to awaken your heart and study your steps. Allow faith swallow up your every fear. God is with you at the break of day. He will not fail you. Though darkness and fear and weakness threaten to overtake you, they will not, they cannot, because you belong to Jesus. He is your stronghold, your high tower, your deliverer, and your defender. He heals, reveals, corrects, and redirects. He's your good shepherd and will lead you safely through the storm. Trust Him with your whole heart today.

July 7

Allow yourself to hear and ponder what God is saying to you in this place of not-yets and what-ifs. Do you hear His whisper to be still and trust Him? You can dream big dreams in the face of your fears. Courageously hold your ground when you'd rather run and hide. Trust your heart's desires to a God who is very much involved, very much in control, very much interested, and very much invested in your life. Remember who you are. Remember whose you are. Keep perspective. Lay hold of faith. Take the next step. Walk forward in faith, not looking back in fear. You are not finished with your journey.

July 8

There are times of suffering: suddenly and at all different levels. It hits us all in some way, different levels and times. No pain, no difficulty if you're spiritual. Belittled by others when suffering or times of trouble sets people up to confuse and not trust God. Problems do happen, sufferings come, tragedy is a reality. We all have experienced it. Suffering is actually scriptural. The Word is filled with suffering, persecution, doubt, sickness, sorrow."The righteous live by their faith..." We have a hope in Christ Jesus that gives us the assurance He is with us in our suffering, He is capturing our tears, He comforts us in our heartbreak. He gives us strength through our suffering, He heals our pain, He causes our tragedies to become triumphs. Why do we go through these things? How long do we have to suffer? What did I do to cause this? You may say, "I am worn out from groaning and weeping." You are not forsaken or forgotten. We are still HIS and HE has us in the palm of HIS hand. There will be beauty rising from the ashes; hope rises from the pain; strength comes from suffering. Hold on, hold strong, hold fast, dig deep, and hold HIM. When we can't see His hand...we must trust His heart.

July 9

May you embrace the grace to be a work in progress. Look for joy in the journey even while you wait for your breakthrough. Smile at the thought of God's nearness even though you can't always sense His presence. Raise your hands in praise declaring that God has been good, and He'll be good again. Others will marvel at the intimate way you walk with God. Allow your faith to inspire them to lay hold of His sacred invitation to know Him deeply. How blessed you are! Have a great day!

July 10

May you stand strong in the face of enemy threats. Remain confident even when an army rises up against you. Put your flag in the ground and declare that if God is for you, who can stand against you? Far greater is HE who is in you, than he who is in the world. You are God's beloved, and He will guard and guide you, shelter and provide for you, bless and establish you. Jesus loves you and nothing and no one can change His mind about you. He's sold on the idea of you! Live like you're His because you are! When you can't sense what God is up to, trust even more because His heart shines toward you. When your journey is different than you would choose, see His invitation to make you "new." When the storm rages overhead, know—with everything in you—that new mercies are on the other side. When you're tempted to overstate your problems and understate His promises, step back and find your footing again on Christ the solid rock. Stand while all other ground is sinking sand. He is mighty to save, and He is doing a new and beautiful thing in you! Embrace a joy-perspective this day, even though the storms may rage and the unexpected happens, because He is still in control. Have faith, hold your head high, love life, dance in the midst of the raging waves. God has you. Blessings for a relaxing, laughter filled, restful day.

July 11

How are our decisions formed? What drives us to make a decision to go this way or that? Are our decisions determined by how we were raised, whether a positive or neglected childhood? Are our decisions determined by the current culture, economy or others' opinions? When you're weary and tired, allow God to give you rest and a right perspective. At times, our decisions are determined when we are weary and tired, with a give-up mentality. When you long to run ahead on your own, may He give you divine wisdom to wait on Him. Keep listening to His voice and place faith in Him to drive your decisions. When your guard is down and you're vulnerable to the enemy's schemes, feel God protect you and deliver you on every side. During times of fatigue and weariness, it's easy to make wrong decisions. Our faith and dependence on Him will be revealed daily in how we live our life. When you're ready to fly, He lift you up and bless you before a watching world. Take one humble step at a time. Keep depending on Him, He's faithful, He'll lead you to your next place of promise. May deep peace be yours today.

July 12

May you experience the rest and provision of God where you've only known striving and surviving. Experience God's great strength come to bear where you've only known weakness and frustration. Experience fresh life and hope where you've only known heartbreak and struggle. Jesus is alive and at work in the world today. Allow your life to reflect His redeeming power! Have a bold and beautiful day!

July 13

May you stand strong in the face of enemy threats. Remain confident even when an army rises up against you. Put your flag in the ground and declare that if God is for you, who can stand against you? Far greater is HE who is in you, than he who is in the world. You are God's beloved and He will guard and guide you, shelter and provide for you, bless and establish you. Jesus loves you and nothing and no one can change His mind about you. He's sold on the idea of you! Live like you're His because you are!

July 14

May God remove every doubt and remove every hindrance that keeps you from knowing His love in a way that changes you. He can change every circumstance that sends a lying message to you. He will highlight every trial He's using to train you into a warrior. Remind yourself that all of heaven is on your side. You are very close to His heart. Be assured, you are exactly where He wants you. Continue doing what He has placed in you until He changes your path. You are "no where" by accident. He has a plan and a purpose. He is always working on your behalf, even when His plan is not evident. Be assured, your footsteps have been directed by His divine plan.

JULY 15

In the busyness of your everyday life, dare to scoot a little closer to Jesus, cup your ear, and listen to what He has to say to you. He loves you. He cherishes you. He has hopes for you. He wants to heal you, restore you, and renew you. His truth will set you free. His power will part the waters. His love will heal your soul. His heart for you will make you whole. Lean in today and listen for His voice; it's gentle, powerful, redemptive, and life-giving. He loves you! Have a blessed and beautiful day.

JULY 16

When you're weary and tired, may God give you rest and a right perspective. When you long to run ahead on your own, may He give you divine wisdom to wait on Him. When your guard is down and you're vulnerable to the enemy's schemes, may God protect you and deliver you on every side. And when you're ready to fly, may He lift you up and bless you before a watching world. Take one humble step at a time. He'll lead you to your next place of promise. May deep peace be yours today. Don't lose focus. Don't lose hope. Always remember, your story is still being written!

JULY 17

May God give you faith to put fear under your feet. Know that for every way the enemy comes against you, the Lord has a promise to bless you, empower you, and to help you stand strong. Fix your eyes on Jesus and set your heart on His word. Know this: when the enemy comes in like a flood, the Lord will raise up a standard against him. Though storms rage all around us, He will protect and give peace in the middle of the storm. He might not come when the lightning flashes, He might not come when the thunder rolls, but you will know when His spirit's passing because it's that still small voice that will shake your soul. Trust in God, raise your shield, and walk forward in faith. Blessings on your day today!

JULY 18

May Jesus transform you from the inside out. Allow Him to heal your soul and make you whole. He is the Holy One who gave you emotions to feel, hurt, laugh, and cry. He will see you are comforted and will rejoice with you. Toss the taste for the things that weaken you and develop a desire for what's good for your heart, mind, will, emotions and soul. Learn what you need to know, say what you need to say, and pray with humble assurance, because God is good and loves to have conversations with you. Run the race to win, for we are more than conquerors. May you have a blessed and beautiful day.

JULY 19

In this world of identity theft being experienced on a daily basis, let us remember, we have the assurance we are created to be who

God intended. No one can steal our identity in Christ Jesus. We hear about identity theft of private and personal information, thieves using our information to obtain credit, employment, and even medical care. Speaking in the spiritual rather than physical sense of identity theft, who have we allowed to steal our spiritual and emotional identity. Remember, He gave us our identity and the powers of the enemy cannot steal that. We were given a name by our parents; thieves may steal the name but cannot steal our uniqueness in Him. Remember we are not defined by what others say or how they treat us. Remember we are not defined by where we work, where we live, or where we are from. Remember He, the Creator of the Universe, defines us. Remember we were created for a purpose, and we are still in a process. The thief of our souls comes to steal, kill, and destroy...but God secures our worth and will always validate our worth. Have a blessed and worth-filled day.

JULY 20

May God's opinion matter far more to you than man's opinion. Allow His dreams for you to speak louder than your fears. Refuse to read into situations that make you anxious. His promise to protect and provide is enough for you. His forgiveness washes over every sin from your past. Don't ever forget, your past is the past. Lessons learned, but God has a bright new future ahead. Live today with the assurance, your journey is just beginning. Rise up in the knowledge that He's made you brand new, through and through. No spot or stain on you!

JULY 21

Suffering from sickness, illnesses, tragedies, natural disasters, pandemics, and COVID-19, we all manage it differently. Reacting to sufferings...

some blame God, some get closer to Him, some isolate themselves and hold it all in. Sufferings produce perseverance. Be assured there is the opposite of suffering, and it is victory. Strength comes from our weakness. Beauty comes out of the ashes of the fire we've been through. Grace comes from the unimaginable tragedy we endured. Suffering is a battleground, but God gives us the victory. Challenges bring maturity. Prayer brings power. Faith comes out of fear. Inconsolable weeping brings comfort. Weakness brings undeniable strength. We cannot stay in the focus if we don't know the why's, the how's, the when's, the where's and the what's next. Remember He who began a good thing will never leave us without a source of rescue and help. Walk this day and each day in confidence, He has a great plan.

July 22

May you cast your cares on Jesus. Feel your load instantly lighter as you trust in Him. Allow Him to fill you with joy overflowing, right here, right now, right in the midst of your circumstances. Seek the Kingdom power to upstage every worry and every fear. The Kingdom authority helps you to rise above your circumstances instead of being crushed by them. New days are ahead. Breakthrough days are just around the corner. Don't give up hope. You serve the God of the breakthrough, and He is for you. Blessings are in store for you today!

July 23

Pain? Regret? Allow the Lord to dig up the stones of pain, regret, and torment from your soil and deliver you once and for all. Let Him turn over the soil of your heart and plant new seeds of faith, vision, and purpose specific to your life's calling. He will heal those deep places that nag you. He heals those secrets that hurt only you and He knows your pain. Allow Him to restrain you when you feel overwhelming self-condemnation rising up. Let Him show you how important and precious you are. If you allow, He will reveal just how complete you are to Him. He will strengthen those weak places that leave you feeling vulnerable. Today, allow Him to overwhelm you with a fresh revelation of His love so you can believe that nothing is impossible with God on your side!

JULY 24

May you look up from your everydayness with a new expectancy that God is up to something good and new in your life. Allow yourself to sense His love in a fresh way and begin praying with boldness, confidence and conviction. Dare to believe that new things are just around the corner and that God has prepared them specifically for you. Trust Him to heal your soul and make you whole. He invites you to live intimately with Him and abundantly because of Him. Trust Him with your next steps and have a beautiful day.

JULY 25

Has your confidence ever been shaken? Has your spirit ever been broken? I remember growing up and my daddy training animals, whether it was a horse, hunting dogs, or one of my many pets. He would always remind me, each time, every time…never break their spirit. He would remind me, when a spirit is broken, they will never be the same. Be assured on a whole new level of how much God loves you and that He's constantly working on your behalf. Feel a fresh surge of confidence in the middle of your circumstances because you know that God is ultimately in control, and nothing escapes His notice. Never let fear be your master. Be confident to take the next step, even if it's out of your comfort zone. He's equipped you to be mighty in battle. And, in every hardship there are treasures and spoils with your name on them. Walk bravely and confidently today and remember, never let anyone break your spirit. We may be crushed, but not destroyed. We may be cast down, but not cast out. We may have persecution, but we are never abandoned. Feel His protection today.

JULY 26

Have you stepped out onto a ledge, sometimes unknowingly, rebelliously, out of daring or simply out of a sense of adventure? At what point did you realize you've made a huge mistake or misstep and need rescuing? Do you realize, when you step out on the ledge, God is always there to support and catch you? When you fail and falter, He is there. In spite of our mistakes and missteps, failings and falters, God's love and provision more than protects and covers us. In your weakness, experience abounding grace that makes you divinely strong. Where you've experienced loss and brokenness, know healing, wholeness, and redemption. Our Redeemer is for you. He is strong and able to pull you from the ledge and keep you safe on this day and every day.

JULY 27

May God release a fresh favor over your life today. Walk through His opened doors of opportunities and connect with people who see what He sees in you! Respond to the gentle whisper of His Spirit and go where He sends you. Rely on His voice to take you to your next place of promise. Realize, when life, careers, hopes, and dreams change, He orders our steps. Realize when life and our future is uncertain, He has a plan. Take one-day-at-a-time, enjoy each moment as they come and enjoy life. Allow Him to refine your character and redefine what "success" is supposed to look like for you. Remember what "success" looks like for someone else is not what "success" looks like for you. Find joy and fulfillment in your work; find peace in your rest; and be fruitful in everything you put your hand upon. You are a divinely anointed, appointed, heir of Almighty God. Walk in faith every step of the way! Have a blessed day today!

July 28

May peace flow like a river through the very depths of your being. Feel joy rise within you like the morning sun. Allow joy to strengthen and awaken your heart and steady your steps. Allow faith swallow up your every fear. God is with you at the break of day. He will not fail you. Though darkness and fear and weakness threaten to overtake you, they will not, they cannot, because you belong to Jesus. He is your stronghold, your high tower, your deliverer, and your defender. He heals, reveals, corrects, and redirects. Don't let fear prevail when He begins redirecting your steps. He's your very good shepherd and will lead you safely through the storm. Trust Him with your whole heart today.

July 29

We can count on one thing, the same God who never fails is working all things out. God gives you faith to put fear under your feet. Know that for every way the enemy comes against you, the Lord has a promise to bless you to help you stand strong in your confidence and faith. Stand strong on His word. May you fix your eyes on Jesus and set your heart on His word. Know that when the enemy comes in like a flood, the Lord will raise up a standard against him. Trust Him, He knows what He's doing. Remember to breathe and live with expectancy of the promises He has made. Be strong, hopeful, and courageous! Step, walk, and move forward in faith today.

July 30

May you ponder what God is saying to you in this place of "not-yets" and "what-ifs." Do you hear His whisper to be still and trust Him? Dream big dreams in the face of your fears. Courageously hold your ground when you'd rather run and hide. Entrust your heart's desires to a God who is very much involved, very much in control, and very much invested in your life. Remember who you are. Remember whose you are. Keep perspective. Lay hold of faith. Take the next step in faith.

July 31

May you allow God to work in the circumstances that come unexpectedly. Allow God the freedom to guide you through the storms of life. Hurricanes we've experienced, winds that raged, the rains with torrential downpours, the loud thunder and the lightning horrific, we see multi-levels of a hurricane. Yet, in the eye of the hurricane, there is a false sense of calm, serenity and maybe even a little bit of sunshine. The back end of the storm returns. Our lives can mimic a hurricane storm. Know that God is there for us from the beginning, during, and after the storm. We may ask why, how and what, but God has those answers. Seek God to give you peace when life throws you in the middle of a hurricane. Listen to that still small voice in the middle of life's tragedy. God might not come when the lightning flashes, He might not come when the thunder rolls, but you can know that His spirit's passing when you hear that still small voice that will shake your soul. God is always with us on every life's journey. He is in control...today and every day.

Don't lose focus. Don't lose hope. Always remember, your story is still being written.

DON'T LOSE FOCUS.

DON'T LOSE HOPE.

ALWAYS REMEMBER,

YOUR STORY IS STILL BEING WRITTEN.

Write Notes:

__/__/__

Write Notes:

__/__/__

August

AUGUST 1

When the day has been overwhelming and you feel you can't go on, God can lead you beside still waters and provide rest for your weary soul. He sets your thinking in the right direction when you're thinking wrong. He restores your faith and wants you to embrace the "you" He's making you to be. He gives you wisdom to stand and fight when your promised land needs you to stand firm. You have everything you need in Him. Delight in God's rich blessings this day!

AUGUST 2

After a long weary day, find peace in this personal prayer. "Lord, I'm weary after a long day. I lift my chin and look to You. I offer You the cares from the day, the concerns of my heart, and the things that keep me up at night. Take my sincere yet imperfect offerings and miraculously multiply them to meet the needs around me. When I crawl under the covers tonight, help me to remember that I'm not under my circumstances. I'm safe under the shadow of Your wing. Cover me with sweet, nourishing sleep tonight. Oh, how I love You. In Jesus's name I pray to you. Amen."

AUGUST 3

When is enough, enough? Daily we are overwhelmed with advertisements by television, telemarketing, print advertising, mail flyers, social media, and the list goes on-and-on. When are we going to find enough? There is absolutely nothing wrong with having nice things, but all that stuff can rob your peace of mind. Only He can satisfy our deepest desires. Only He can satisfy our hopes. Only He can fill the empty spaces of our hearts. Only He can give us comfort and peace that nothing or no one can. Only He can make a way when there seems to be no way. Only He can make us content when the world is spinning out of control. When we allow Him to become our enough, He will supply the "stuff" we need for our physical needs. Allow Him in your heart and allow Him to become your "enough."

AUGUST 4

May the Lord Himself establish you in His highest and best purposes for you. He opens doors, move mountains, and bring provision in the very near future just for you. Confirm your faith steps and energize your prayers through Him. He is mighty, He is good, and He cares about every detail of your life. Obey Him and do what He says. He's making a way where there is no way. He loves you truly and deeply. Trust Him today and every day. He will make a way when there seems to be no way. When you can't see His hand, trust His heart. He is there for you today and all days!

AUGUST 5

Have you ever seen someone fall or possibly fallen yourself? Have your feet ever tangled in a rug, and you did a dance attempting to stay upright? Have you ever grabbed something to keep from falling? We all have. What about a life-altering event that comes from nowhere? What about the unexpected loss of a loved one, the unexpected medical diagnosis, a spouse throwing their hands up and walking out, or the loss of a long-time career? As the media has kept us informed of the pandemic, protests, political fighting, and tragedies in our country and globally, we just can't imagine the horrific damages unfolding in the middle of these tragic events. No one expects the rug to be yanked out from under them; life-changing events usually don't announce themselves. See through the storm. Daily, we are on a journey of uncertainty, but also of hope and life. Faith and hope are ours in Christ. He will never leave us. Nothing takes Him by surprise. He will walk with us daily and hold our hand through the emotional roller coaster. He will wipe our tears and He hears our silent cries. Our journey is not always easy... but you are not alone.

"It is your own convictions which compels you; that is, choice compels choice." – Epictetus, Greek Philosopher

AUGUST 6

Let's wrap our arms around the ones we love, look them in the eyes, and tell them how much they are treasured. Look around, take notice, and give thanks for all your blessings. When you're tempted to indulge in melancholy or discontentment, raise your hands, and thank God for His daily and divine intervention. We don't have the answers to why or when tragedy happens, BUT we do have the assurance God will be there with us every day and every step of the journey. Hold onto faith and family, like never before. We only get one chance at this thing called life, so hold on tight. We may not see family as often as we like, yet we remain close and strong. Humble gratitude give us spiritual insight. In a world of chaos and hatefulness, just be kind and share your God-given love with a smile today.

AUGUST 7

"I can bring life; I can bring death. I can bring peace; I can bring dismay. I can promote, I can destroy. I can lift up; I can tear down. I can be heard but not seen. What am I?" The answer to this riddle: Words…just words. Words have to be chosen carefully. Speak your words to lift up, promote, encourage, help, give hope, be full of empathy, and compassion. It takes a moment to choose whether we will use our words wisely or allow our words to destroy. Words are powerful. Let your words be faith builders and not words that incite fear. Be someone's "superhero." Remember once a moment is gone, we can never recapture that moment to cancel words spoken. Speak wisely. Your words should always be acceptable to Him. Speak kind and faith-filled words today.

AUGUST 8

May you refuse condemnation for the ways you fail and fall short in your everyday life. Instead, embrace God's relentless grace that covers you from head to toe. Entrust your whole soul and story to Jesus so you can fully enjoy your journey with Him. He's not disgusted by your weaknesses, He's moved by them, and He treasures you. Shake off your regrets and grab a firm hold of God's promise to forgive, restore, and renew your story. Other's opinions no longer tie you up in knots because God's opinion continually sets you free from their negativity. Determine with all your heart to live the abundant, powerful, forgiven life Jesus offers you. Lean into the soul-stirring, heart-freeing grace that

Jesus purchased just for you. Walk fully assured that Jesus has you close to His heart. Feel uplifted on this day.

AUGUST 9

Is it a relationship or religion? People have their own perception of who or what God is. Sometimes we rely more on reasoning, science, knowledge, opinions of who He is. Who is He to you? What has He revealed to you? How have you been hurt by those who misrepresent who He is? There have been times during our ministry and even our secular lives, hurts have been inflicted by those who "knew" Him or "felt" they had a word from Him. Perception leads to falsely concerted knowledge and ignorance of the real truth. We cannot totally be dependent on our own reasonings and assumptions because knowledge puffs up, but love builds up. Challenge yourself to find Him for yourself. Build your perception of His truthful knowledge and love. Culture is always calling us to be this or that...but God wants us to be who He wants us to be and all we can be in Him. Don't let culture define your perception, allow Him to define our perception. Seek Him today.

AUGUST 10

As you step back and survey the parts of your life that break your heart or things that don't make sense right now, stand strong, look up, and consider what God's resurrection "power" can do in, through you for you, and around you. Only those who've walked through the "valley of the shadow" will truly grasp the power of redemption on the other side. Jesus withholds no good thing from those who walk intimately with Him. He's not the reason you suffer; He's with you in the storm. He is your shelter, deliverer, and strong tower. He's Your redeemer, savior, and friend. He's your Prince of Peace and Sure Defender. Find your footing again. Engage your faith. Embrace the right perspective. Trust Jesus with your whole heart and see what High love will do for you today and all days.

AUGUST 11

Cultivate a heart that knows how to be thankful for the breathtaking moments. Though storms rage all around us, we know the One who calms the storm. Take every chance you get to spend time with God, think about His love, and trust His direction in your life. As you look to Him, your entire perspective will change. Through you, others will be reminded that there's a God in heaven very much involved in the smallest details of our lives. Take time to look around and enjoy…life. Embrace a joy-filled, faith-filled, hope-filled, renewed perspective today and each day.

AUGUST 12

Have you ever given or accepted a dare? We all have, especially as children. We believed we could manage anything, we knew more than our parents, and we were invincible. We did not realize the dangers lurking around us and how God was always protecting us. Dare yourself to trust in the Lord with your whole heart, and not lean on your own understanding. Look up and acknowledge Him with every step you take, knowing He'll get you where you need to go. Have hope in Him and not in the approval of man. Believe Him for a beautiful outcome even though it's tempting to lose hope. Hope in Him will never disappoint. He loves you more than you can even comprehend. Trust Him with your heart and soon your eyes will see how good He is. Blessings as you take on the dare of Trusting Him.

AUGUST 13

No matter what you're going through, remember that your identity is secure in Christ; it's not up for grabs or changeable with popular opinion. Remember, He is your source. When you are being shut out, pushed out, excluded, verbally attacked, don't despair...Jesus loves how He made you! He is the only validation you need. Trust Him to guide, provide, direct, and even redirect you along the way. Your hope is in the Lord. Allow faith to carry you even when you can't find a reason for hope. In life, seasons come, and seasons go, people come, and people go, but God's love for you is abundant, profound, and amazingly real, right here, right now, and never leaves you. Walk like you're loved because you are beyond your wildest dreams. Have a beautiful day!

AUGUST 14

May you allow Jesus to woo you away from the distractions and chaos of this world, leading you to quiet waters so you can rest and refresh, for as long as it takes. He breathes fresh life into your soul and feel fresh healing to your hurts. Sense His hands on your face and hear Him speak words of truth, affection, and redemption over you. Be aware of His love and how it makes every lesser enticement fade away. He is your faithful defender, your most loyal friend, your greatest advocate. The relationship with Him is the highest of all goals and prizes. He is yours and you are His, truly and undoubtedly. Live every single day with the awareness of His presence. He's with you. You have everything you need.

AUGUST 15

Perspective is in the eye of the beholder. Perspective is seen differently according to the side of the road you're on. Let us realize God is the one who can give us a clear perception of right and wrong, of hope and peace, love and compassion. The Lord Himself gives you a fresh perspective on your life. Begin to see your troubles, difficult as they are, as growth and development moments. Wrap your arms around the promise that those very troubles are achieving for you, an eternal glory that far outweighs everything else. Jesus is deeply invested in your journey and intends to get you safely home. He goes before you, He has your back, and He puts His hand of blessing upon your head. He can give you a glimpse of glory, a peek into the eternal significance of your life because He is doing glorious work in and through you. You matter deeply to Him. May your spirit be renewed in His presence today!

AUGUST 16

Have you ever heard the wind whisper your name? Have you ever heard your name whispered by a loved one who left us long ago? The Lord calls our name, and it is such a beautiful, quiet whisper. You grow to love the sound of God's voice in your ear. Cultivate a heart of peace and a heart at rest that you fully trust your Father to lead you in the way that you should go. Lose your taste for the things that weaken you. Develop a hunger and a thirst for all God has for you. You can receive a fresh revelation of God's love and promise for you. You are a gifted, treasured, loved person and you're called to impact the world in a way that only you can. Allow the love of Christ comfort and compel you in the days ahead. He wants to open your eyes to the new opportunities ahead of you. Blessings on your day today!

AUGUST 17

Have you ever come to a place on the road you're traveling with a sudden detour sign with no advance warning? In this world of discontent, distractions, disillusionment, despondency, despairing, and detours, we can be assured we can always look up. He is always there with us, and for us. This world is disquieting, and we have daily disappointments daily. Detours don't always mean denial to our destination, but they can be moments of learning. We may see something we've never seen before. Be assured, delay doesn't mean denial. Detours are not indications of danger ahead. When our journey seems, there is no right or left turn, and we can neither go forward and we never want to go backward, God is there. He is with us on the journey. He will guide us. When we can't see his hand, trust His still small voice that whispers, guiding us and leading us on the right path. The road may be filled with detours, but they are always for a purpose. He is always protecting us. He orders our footsteps. Trust Him. He will never let you down.

AUGUST 18

Do have low self-esteem, lack of confidence, or feel an uncertainty of acceptance in a new environment? I challenge you to refuse to feel unworthy. You're established for Jesus's namesake. You are loved, treasured, appointed, and anointed. You are a person of quality and worth, so never allow anyone to diminish your value. You're free to climb mountain heights with joy and free to stumble and fall without condemnation. I challenge you to refuse to fall in the trap of self-condemnation and even though words of others do hurt, those words do not define who we are and are supposed to be. Our destinies are not defined by jealousy and envy, but by God's Word. Know that you are capable of more than you think you are. Jesus holds your present and future. Know His love, truly and deeply. Trust His heart. Above all else, be yourself. And do only what He asks and leads you to do. Have a blessed, prosperous, confident-filled day.

AUGUST 19

Take cues from God, and not from culture, to become a powerful, praying saint. Dream those big dreams with God. Pray prayers that make your knees buckle and your heart tremble as you entrust your whole soul and story to the God of the Universe. He intends to solve some of the world's problems through you. When the enemy comes in like a flood, the Lord raises a standard against him. This is no time for cowering in fear. This is a time to rise up in faith! Trust God's Word. Believe His promises. Do what He says. And in due time, you'll see the 'waters' part, the mountains move, and the answers you've been waiting for. You are mighty in God. Walk full-of-faith today.

AUGUST 20

Allow God to lift your chin, awaken your heart, and open your eyes to all you possess in Him. Refuse to let your disappointments define you. Stand on that barren land and envision a harvest. Experience a revival of faith in the very place of your heartbreak. Instead of rehashing your losses, rehearse His promises because they're truer than your circumstances. Today's a good day to embrace faith, to give thanks, and to worship the One who keeps His promises. You've got everything you need in Him. Have a blessed day.

AUGUST 21

The way. The truth. The life. Jesus is the Way. His word is truth that will never lead us astray. His word will make a way when there seems to be no way. He is the life that gives us hope in the middle of suffering. He transforms our lives. Cultivate a lifestyle that creates space for grace, growth, and transformation. A complete metamorphosis of every part of your life. Guard against toxic thoughts, attitudes, and mindsets that only weaken you. Fill your thoughts with all that's lovely, praiseworthy, truthful, and life filled. In the days ahead, walk with Jesus, exemplify your love, and renew your prayers. He will guide you in your decisions. Guard your thoughts, focus and hide His words in your heart and it'll change your life. You are on an ongoing transformation...always progressing.

AUGUST 22

Before you take another step today, pause and give your burdens to Jesus. He'll carry what's too heavy for you. He'll give you grace to shoulder the light and easy yoke that fits you perfectly. Discern the worries that slow you down and make life unnecessarily burdensome. Choose the discipline of joy and discover a new strength in the process. Embrace grace for the moment, power in prayer, and perspective with the story God is writing in your life. You're loved, called, cherished, anointed, and appointed. Refuse yesterday's baggage, tomorrow's worries, or today's insecurities. When life throws you a curve ball and the unexpected happens, remember that you've got Jesus and He's got you. Find certainty in Him, and in this world of uncertainties, be assured. He is with you always.

AUGUST 23

As you entrust your cares and concerns to God, refuse the temptation to fixate on the signs and symptoms that cause you angst and worry. Instead of praying to God and then continually peeking at your circumstances, seek His face, and then press on to know His heart. Become confident in His attention to detail, be assured of His great love for you, and enjoy your life until the breakthrough comes. Even when the wind blows and you feel you're going under, keep your eyes on Him; He'll hold you up. Embrace His promises. Enjoy your life. And have confidence in Him. God will move on your behalf in the days to come!

AUGUST 24

As the day wraps up and you crawl into bed tonight, may your body, mind, and soul be at rest and know the deep, abiding peace that comes from deeply knowing God. Listen and He will speak to you while you sleep. Welcome His fresh insight and perspective regarding your current circumstances. As you rise up in the morning, allow faith rise up in you and compel you to obey when you'd rather self-protect, give when you'd rather hoard, and trust when you're tempted to worry. You're not made for this place. His plan is to restore you, strengthen you, and for you to have a brand-new peace-filled day.

AUGUST 25

May God's peace mark your day in every way. When the Lord shows you the places in your life where you've let your guard down, don't let your thoughts wander or let your heart grow weary. Allow Him to validate your existence. Allow Him to renew your mind and perspective. Allow yourself to walk with Him intimately and confidently. His highest and best purposes are for your good. Ignore the enemy. Refuse indulgences that weaken you. Engage in all of the things that are good for your soul. Jesus loves you and He wants what's best for you. Have a peace-saturated day today!

AUGUST 26

Never judge someone by another's opinion. Kindness is free. A smile costs nothing. Encouragement is free. A look in the eye and smile can begin something beautiful. Pray that God gives you kindness and grace for those who step on your toes and talk negatively about you. Allow Him to give you holy and humble confidence in the presence of those who misunderstand you. He will give you love and forgiveness to those who hurt you. Allow His love to spill over you until you're confident you are everything to Him. Be an "ambassador" for kindness today.

AUGUST 27

There is only one solution to the chaos, anxiety, strife, and uncertainty in this world. Our hope, our encouragement, our answer, our assurance and our confidence is in Him. When we feel overwhelmed, alone, forsaken, forlorn, abandoned, disillusioned, and discouraged, Jesus Christ is our everything. You are never alone. When our foundation is shaken and rocked to the core, He is there. He is the solid, firm, and sustainable foundation we can always hold onto. He assured us, the foundation built on Him will never disintegrate beneath us. When our journey appears to be all bad, He is with us. When our journey feels like nothing can go wrong, He is with us. Good or bad, He reassures us that we are never forgotten. When you can't see His hand, trust His heart. Today, decide to be who He says you are and can be.

AUGUST 28

No matter what you're going through, remember that your identity is secure in Christ. It's not up for grabs or changeable with popular opinion. Jesus loves how He made you. Trust Him to guide, provide, correct, and redirect you along the way. Love people but keep your hope in the Lord. Find faith when you can't find a reason for hope. Seasons come and seasons go, but God's love for you is abundant, profound, and amazingly real, right here, right now. Embrace you He's made. He gives you wisdom and strength. Be strong and know you have everything you need in Him. May your day be blessed!

AUGUST 29

May Jesus put your heart at ease this very moment. Encounter His peace in a way you never have before. Allow joy spring up in your soul where you've only known worry and frustration. Know the struggles that have plagued you are small in the light of God's very real and personal love for you. Jesus will give you a glimpse of His glory, just enough to remind you that you're not walking this road alone. Live by faith and not by sight, and it's sometimes good for the soul to see what our heart already knows. God will allow you to see just enough to put your soul at ease and your heart at rest. God is good that way. Invite Him to move in close and be your strength today.

AUGUST 30

May you be diligent about taking time to pause and reflect on the many ways God has blessed you. Though storms rage all around us, we know the One who calms the storm. Take every chance you get to spend time with God, think about His love, and trust His direction in your life. As you look to Him, your whole countenance will change, and others will be reminded that there's a God in heaven and very much involved in our lives. Others will see and feel your God given peace. Embrace a joyful, faith-filled perspective today!

AUGUST 31

Can you dare to trust in the Lord with your whole heart, and not lean on your own understanding? Look up and acknowledge Him with every step you take, knowing He'll get you where you need to go. Put your hope in Him and not in the approval of man. Believe Him for a beautiful outcome even though it's tempting to lose hope. Hope in Him will never disappoint. He loves you more than you can even comprehend. Trust Him with your heart. You will feel His goodness. Blessings on your day today!

DON'T LOSE FOCUS.

DON'T LOSE HOPE.

ALWAYS REMEMBER,

YOUR STORY IS STILL BEING WRITTEN.

Write Notes:

__/__/__

September

SEPTEMBER 1

May the Lord dig up the stones of pain, regret, and angst from your soil and deliver you once and for all. Allow Him to turn over the soil of your heart and plant new seeds of faith, vision, and purpose specific to your life's calling. Feel His healing those deep places that nag you. Know that He strengthen those weak places that leave you feeling vulnerable. He will overwhelm you with a fresh revelation of His love so you can believe and know that nothing is impossible with God on your side! Have a faith-filled day.

SEPTEMBER 2

Sometimes, in our lives, we feel like we are rotten inside, unusable, no longer fresh, vibrant, needed or wanted? God gives us the assurance by His instilling that small voice in our ears. Instinctively you know you'll be okay. With new hope that springs within our souls, we realize we are not like the potato that needs to be trashed. Just when we think it's over, God takes his pen and writes more of our story. He shows us that it's our time for the world to see that dark, rotten place we've gone through, was allowed only to sprout growth and the development of His plan. Be assured you are wanted and needed. Have a peace-saturated day today!

September 3

May God's peace mark your day in every way. Don't become weary in doing what's right, honorable, and ethical. Be assured, our labor is not in vain. Realize there are physical, mental, emotional, and spiritual laboring. If we labor with integrity and character, The Creator of the Universe will continue to bless, sustain and keep us strong. With Him, solidify your life once again. With Him, renew your mind and perspective. With Him, walk intimately and turn a deaf ear to the enemy. Refuse indulgences that weaken you. Engage in all of the things that are good for your soul. Jesus loves you and He wants what's best for you. Walk in God powered strength today.

September 4

May you see the wisdom of preparing a resting heart especially when the world rages in the storm. Embrace the insight to notice holy-ground moments in your everyday life. Take off your shoes and slow your pace even though others race past you. Open up your spirit-filled eyes to the fact that God is on His throne. He has not looked away, and He will one day break through and redeem your story. Jesus will fill you with a new dose of holy confidence and humble dependence so that so you can walk in wisdom in and run the race to win. Enjoy His plan and journey for you today and each day.

September 5

May you believe that your wildest God-given dreams can come true. Trust Jesus enough to follow Him through the valley to lay hold of them. Be patient and purposeful. Put aside selfish ambition and allow holy ambition to arise. Lean in to your "self-purposed-quiet" time, so you'll be prepared and strengthened to stand in your next place of promise. Poised yourself to be guided. Embrace a positive force for change. Be determined to see the good when others see the bad. Make a conscious decision to be mindfully kind. Open your eyes to see hope when all hope seems gone. Be assured that every step is determined by God.

September 6

May you find shelter beneath the shadow of God's wing. Be wise enough to stay in His established space for you, trusting He'll move you to your next place when the timing is right. His grace will empower you to live abundantly, to stand strong, and to pray powerfully. Your honor for Him will compel you to trust Him when your trials seem truer than His word. He will not fail you, will not forget about you, and will not turn away from you. He's with you in battle, He'll help you when your heart breaks, and He'll deliver you and bless you before a watching world when the time is right. Trust Him. You're so very dear to His heart. Have a grace-filled day!

September 7

May peace flow like a river through the very depths of your being. Let joy rise within you like the morning sun. Feel the strength awaken your heart and sturdy your steps. Allow faith swallow up your every fear. God is with you at the break of day. He will not fail you. Though darkness and fear and weakness threaten to overtake you, they will not, they cannot, because you belong to Jesus. He is your stronghold, your high tower, your deliverer, and your defender. He heals, reveals, corrects, and redirects. He's your very good shepherd and will lead you safely through the storm. Trust Him with your whole heart today.

SEPTEMBER 8

May you look up and remember once again that the Lord is your very dear and precious shepherd. Because you have Him, you have everything you need. He causes you to lie down and rest, He leads you to still waters and sacred spaces to restore your soul. He leads you along the path of righteousness for His namesake. Even when you walk through the deepest valley, He is right there with you, close beside you. He corrects and directs, guides and provides, and He'll never forsake you. He establishes you and honors you in front of your enemies. He pours out a fresh anointing on your life when you need it. He fills your cup to overflowing. His goodness and mercy chases after you and always will. You are blessed because you get to dwell in the house of the Lord all the days of your life.

SEPTEMBER 9

In the busyness of your everyday life, dare to scoot a little closer to Jesus, cup your ear, and listen to what He has to say to you. He loves you. He cherishes you. He has hopes for you. He wants to heal you, restore you, and renew you. His truth will set you free. His power will part the waters. His love will heal your soul. His heart for you will make you whole. Lean in today. Listen for His voice; it's gentle, powerful, redemptive, and life-giving. Oh, how He loves you! May you dare to believe who you can be because of Him. Have a blessed and beautiful day.

SEPTEMBER 10

May God inspire you to achieve a goal that He puts in your heart. Stir up faith as you step up and step out. Allow Him to give you fresh conviction and discipline to say no to lesser things so you can say yes to His best plan for you. Feel the wind of the Holy Spirit fill your sail and take you to a new, inspired place. Put your goals in His hands and allow Him to lead you to achievement. Live today with his lead.

SEPTEMBER 11

This day, heroes emerged from ordinary people. God gave strength to those who thought they were weak. Supernatural strength of the human spirit prevailed. Wrap your arms around this truth: God is with you and it's impossible for Him to fail you! Lean into Jesus today. He's got you. Let us never forget this tragic day when our land was attacked. Continue to pray for those who lost loved ones on 9/11. Keep this day in memory and choose faith today.

SEPTEMBER 12

May you bend your ear toward heaven and listen to Jesus's song over you, for its healing, redemptive, and life-giving. When you're tempted to listen to contrary voices, may God's truth fill your heart and drowned out lesser opinions. You are made in God's image for a divine purpose on the earth today. Even your battles can serve you well if you trust God to train you in them. Nothing can separate you from the Father's fierce love for you. He has set His affection on you and He's not giving up on you! Choose faith in this place today. Right here, right now, wrap your arms around this truth: God is with you and it's impossible for Him to fail you! Lean into Jesus today. He's got you.

SEPTEMBER 13

May God help you be fully present with the ones you love. He will give you discernment not to pass by the sacred moments He supplies. He will give you faith to believe in Him for great things and insight to fully embrace what you already possess in Him. He will overwhelm you with a renewed sense of His very personal love for you. Delight in his presence today!

SEPTEMBER 14

God loves you. He cherishes you. He has hopes for you. He wants to heal you, restore you, and renew you. His truth will set you free. His power will part the waters. His love will heal your soul. His heart for you will make you whole. Lean in today. Listen for His voice—His gentle, powerful, redemptive, and life-giving voice. Believe you can be the person he want you to be because He loves you today and every day.

SEPTEMBER 15

In the days ahead, may you—more and more—die to the power of others' opinions that you may more fully live out of the relentless, abundant love God has for you. As people become crueler and more careless with their opinions, may you become wiser and discerning with yours. Jesus Himself will empower you with grace, ignite you with faith, and overwhelm you with His love. Speak with precision, pray with power, and stand in courage. Your life and influence matter deeply in this desperate world. Lean in and learn everything you can from the One who loves you deeply and intends to use you greatly. Have a blessed and beautiful day!

SEPTEMBER 16

May you be content to know that you cannot be all things to all people; you live to serve an audience of One. Love people but keep your hope in God. Be willing to take risks with people, but may your sole trust be in God. The power you once gave to others rest solely on God because He defines, He saves, He provides, and He has the power to transform. Walk free and full of joy today!

SEPTEMBER 17

May you cast your cares on Jesus. Your load feel instantly lighter as you trust in Him. Jesus will fill you with joy overflowing in the midst of your circumstances. The Kingdom power upstages every worry and every fear. Allow the Kingdom authority to help you to rise above your circumstances instead of being crushed by them. New days are ahead. Breakthrough days are just around the corner. Don't give up hope. You serve the God of the breakthrough, and He is for you. Be bless today!

SEPTEMBER 18

May God grant you abundant grace and a right perspective. Allow Him to instill in your heart and mind new courage to stand strong and think long. In the middle of the storm, remember who you are. As you move forward from this place, pray powerful prayers based on God's goodness and your connection to Him. You're His. He is yours. Dare to stand in faith and hang on until the storm passes. Soon the sun will break through the clouds and Jesus will bring clarity to your situation, spirit and soul. Until then, trust God and remember that He is good even when life is hard. Have a grace-filled day.

SEPTEMBER 19

May the enemy's plan against you backfire as you grow stronger in your trials, not weaker. Your sturdy grasp of God's promises intimidate the enemy and make him lose heart. Find JOY in the heat of the battle, POWER in the promises of God, and PROVISION where you've known lack. All things you once knew of God pale in comparison to what you know of Him now. You are growing stronger. He makes all things new. He breaks through. And He will come through for you. Soldier on, mighty one! God is with you today and every day.

SEPTEMBER 20

May you take time to be with family. Take time to pamper yourself because you are important. Realize that during times of self-reflection, you are loved and cherished. Never compare yourself to the "perfect social media" world of others. You are God's child. He made you to be you. Find deep nourishing rest in being you. Today, may profound times of prayer be yours.

SEPTEMBER 21

When you're weary and tired, may God give you rest and a right perspective. When you long to run ahead on your own, allow Him to give you divine wisdom to wait on Him. When your guard is down and you're vulnerable to the enemy's schemes, feel God's protection for and on you. When you're ready to fly, may He lift you up and bless you before a watching world. Take one humble step at a time. He'll lead you to your next place of promise. Trust God's plans for you and walk in faith.

SEPTEMBER 22

Today, pray this prayer: Jesus, help me to find nourishing rest in You this day. You are greater than my trials, stronger than my emotions, and fiercer than my enemy. You withhold no good thing from those who walk intimately with You. No enemy can defeat You, no storm can diminish You, and no circumstance can distract You. Your promises are true, Your power is sure, and Your love is deep. You are mighty to save, and I am mighty in You. I have all I need and then some. Thank you, Lord.

SEPTEMBER 23

May God surprise you with moments of grace and refreshment. Allow Him to bring the long-awaited breakthrough. Allow Him to bless you with sudden belly laughter and watery-eyed joy. He will give you a gift that you least expect. Seek Him so He can inspire you to pray more audaciously than you ever have before. He is with you and for you. A new and fresh hope will suddenly arise within you. Walk with faith and confidence today.

SEPTEMBER 24

Today's prayer: Lord Jesus open hearts. Forgive us our sins, heal our land, and awaken Godly convictions within us. Open our eyes to the suffering around us, open our ears to more quickly discern Your voice, and change our appetites so we hunger more for the things of God. Crush the wicked, rescue the vulnerable, restore broken marriages, put orphans in families, and bring the wayward back to You. Our only hope is You. Guide me through this day, Lord. Amen.

SEPTEMBER 25

We all know the iconic story of a short cruise becoming a deserted island experience. No matter the plans, diagrams, meetings, or money could get them off the island. There was The Skipper, Gilligan, The Millionaire and his wife, Professor, and Mary Ann all stuck together on an island. Imagine the personalities and differences. Of course, until...the sitcom ended and there was a rescue. There are parallels and analogies from this sitcom to true life today. We may not be on an actual deserted island. However, we can feel isolated, alone, shut out and not included. Sometimes we feel deserted, yet we are never deserted...for God is always with us. I know God has a plan and a purpose; He will never leave us alone. God has our backs, and He includes us in His circle. Walk with Him today. You are not alone.

September 26

May new and fresh hope suddenly arise within you! The enemy's plan against you will backfire as you grow stronger in your trials, not weaker. Place a sturdy grasp around God's promises that intimidate the enemy and make him lose heart. He will come through for you. Soldier on, stay persistent, keep trusting for the rescue. God is with you!

September 27

May you be diligent about taking time to pause and reflect on the many ways God has blessed you. May you cultivate a heart that knows how to rest in God alone. Though storms rage all around us, we know the One who calms the storm. May you take every chance you get to spend time with God, think about His love, and trust His direction in your life. As you look to Him, your whole countenance will change, and others will be reminded that there's a God in heaven very much involved in our lives. He intends to get us safely home. But don't wait 'till then to find rest in Him. Embrace a joyful, faith-filled perspective today.

September 28

May God grace you with a new perspective on an old situation. He will give you fresh faith when you're feeling faint. He will inspire new initiative where you've lost momentum. You will encounter His goodness in the days ahead in a way that forever changes how you walk with God. Don't be afraid, be brave.

September 29

Have you ever, out of the depths of your soul, said, "I'm tired! I'm just tired and can't do this thing anymore? I'm weary? I'm exhausted of this thing called struggle." May God's peace mark your day in every way. Don't become weary in doing what's right, honorable, and ethical. Be assured, our labor is not in vain. Realize there are physical, mental, emotional, and spiritual laboring. If we labor with integrity and character, The Creator of the Universe will continue to bless, sustain, and keep us strong. Allow the Lord to show you places in your life where you've let your guard down, let your thoughts wander, and let your heart grow weary. Allow Him to solidify your life once again. With Him, you can renew your mind and perspective. With Him, you can walk intimately acquainted with His highest and best purposes for you. Turn a deaf ear to the enemy. Refuse indulgences that weaken you. Engage in all of the things that are good for your soul. Jesus loves you and He wants what's best for you. Have a peace-saturated day today!

September 30

When life knocks you down, may you get back up again because greater is He who is in you than he who is in the world! When your rogue emotions turn you upside down, may you find your footing again by standing on the truth of who you are in Christ Jesus. When your perspective dims because the clouds block the sun, God Himself can break through with a fresh perspective on His promises. You are loved, called, cared for, and appointed to be a blessing to a world very much in need. Changeable things in your life will take a back seat to the unchangeable, unfailing love, and faithfulness of God. You're blessed and God has given you a sturdy place to stand. When you think something will turn out one way, it ends with a complete opposite result. Be assured...God is in control...always. Have a great day!

Don't lose focus.

Don't lose hope.

Always remember,

your story is still being written.

Write Notes:

__/__/__

October

OCTOBER 1

May you see the wisdom and power of entrusting your cares to God. When you bow low, He rises up! He will deliver, defend, and establish you. In the meantime, learn to rest in His care, trust in His word, and embrace a joy-filled life. Jesus knows your name, knows where you live. He loves you right here, right now, yesterday-today-forever. He will take you where you need to go. He will reach out to the ones you love. He will validate and vindicate you in His time. See and believe that you're safest when you're at His feet, trusting Him to do what you cannot do for yourself. Allow your soul find rest in Him.

OCTOBER 2

May God give you faith to put fear under your feet. For every way the enemy comes against you, the Lord has a promise to bless you to help you stand strong. Fix your eyes on Jesus and set your heart on His word. Know this: when the enemy comes in like a flood, the Lord will raise up a standard against him. He has you! Walk believing, with a faith-filled mind-set.

October 3

When you're weary and tired, may God give you rest and a right perspective. When you long to run ahead on your own, seek Him to give you divine wisdom and wait on Him. When your guard is down and you're vulnerable to the enemy's schemes, God will protect you and deliver you on every side. When you're ready to fly, allow Him to lift you up and bless you before a watching world. Take one humble step at a time. He'll lead you to your next place of promise.

October 4

May God open the heavens, break through the clouds, and deliver the answer you've been waiting for. He will shore up your faith, strengthen your heart, and overwhelm you with His grace. Your soul will know a peaceful assurance like it's never known before. Believe from deep within that God is with you, for you, and will never let you go. He is mighty to save. Bless assurance is yours!

October 5

May God give you faith to put fear under your feet. Know that for every way the enemy comes against you, the Lord has a promise to bless you, empower you, and to help you stand strong. Fix your eyes on Jesus and set your heart on His word. Know this: when the enemy comes in like a flood, the Lord will raise up a standard against him! Be still and listen for that small voice that will shake your soul. Trust in God, raise your shield, and walk forward in faith! Blessings on your day today!

October 6

May God open your eyes wide to the wonder of His great affection for you. You will suddenly feel, know, and believe that you are deeply loved, abundantly cared for, and profoundly called. Feel your heart awaken to the heavenly resources you've yet to lay hold of. See others with new eyes of compassion and empathy. Give generously as one who has an endless supply to draw from. You are loved, called, equipped, and provided for. Yes, we have faced adversity, troubles, tragedies, difficulties and sufferings...but God is our refuge. Remember in the middle of the difficulty we can, rejoice and live boldly. The Savior has you in His hand and in His heart.

October 7

May your deep desire for God's presence, power and purpose overshadow every negative thing in your life. Be hungry for His holiness that will make you lose your taste for toxic time-wasters. May you desire to see Him move mightily, push you to move outside your comfort zone. Obey Him even when it doesn't suit you. Allow His passion for you to ignite your passion for Him. Nothing compares to knowing the Lord of Angel Armies. He delights in you. Be assured, you are His chosen.

October 8

May you trade your time-wasters for things that nourish your soul and renew your strength. Turn your back on influences that diminish your identity and distract you from your high call in Jesus Christ. Give more time to words, thoughts, and songs that remind you who you are in Jesus. Carefully guard your tastes and preferences, so you don't lose your taste for the things of God. Nothing on this earth and no one else can satisfy our souls' deepest longings like Jesus can. You're made for Him. May you find your purpose in Him.

OCTOBER 9

May you become powerful in God as you wait for your breakthrough. In this "not yet" season, seek to learn the secret of abiding in Him, fortifying your roots deep in His marvelous love, and instinctively trusting that He has your absolute best in mind. Become so acquainted with His word and His presence that you plant seeds of faith for a future harvest. Instead of angst over your "not yet" learn to embrace awe for the reality of your faith, the substance of His promises, and the surety that any day now He will break through. Be pleased that you have a precious heart for Him during this time-in-between. Wait faithfully on Him. What you are waiting for is just around the corner. Don't lose hope during the in between. You are on this journey for a purpose.

OCTOBER 10

Know that God goes before you, and He's got your back. He's there, just around the bend. He'll never forsake you. Trust Him to bring clarity to His future plans for you. Be assured of a greater level of His deep love for you and of His intimate attention to detail. As He bids you to come, let go of what feels safe. Lay hold of the new place He has for you. He's doing a new thing; don't hang on to the old just because you know it so well. Don't miss out on the invitation. He bids you come. Take the next step in faith and follow what is set in front of you. May today be your purpose-filled day in Him.

OCTOBER 11

May you have the presence of mind to cherish every second with the ones you love. May you make time for fun, for rest, and for reflection. Plan time in your schedule not to have plans and see what happens. Come to know—on a whole new level—that much more rests on God shoulders than on yours. Learn to enjoy the journey because His yoke is easy, and His burden is light. He loves you and He is in control.

OCTOBER 12

May God lift your chin, awaken your heart, and open your eyes to all you possess in Him. Refuse to let your disappointments define you. Instead, stand on that barren land and envision a harvest. Experience a revival of faith. Instead of rehashing your losses, decide to rehearse His promises because they're truer than your circumstances. Today embrace faith, give thanks, and worship the One who keeps His promises. Jesus loves you and He is faithful to His word. May His love define you and His promises hem you in and shore you up. You've got everything you need in Him.

OCTOBER 13

May Jesus Himself woo you away from the distractions of this world and lead you to quiet waters so you can rest awhile. Allow Him to breathe fresh life into your soul and fresh healing to your hurts. Sense His hands on your face and hear Him speak works of truth, affection, and redemption over you. Become aware of His love that makes every lesser affection fade away. He is your highest aim, your most lofty goal, your greatest prize. You have Him. Live every single day with the awareness of His presence. He's with you. You have everything you need. Enjoy blessings on this day!

October 14

When you can't sense what God is up to, is the time you trust even more. Feel His heart lean towards you. When your journey is different than you would choose, respond to His invitation to make you anew. When the storm rages overhead, know that new mercies are on the other side. When you're tempted to overstate your problems and understate His promises, step back and find your footing again. Christ is the solid rock you stand while all other ground is sinking sand. He is mighty to save, and He is doing a new and beautiful thing in you! May today be your breakthrough-solid-ground revelation kind of day!

October 15

May you stretch out your arms, open your hands, and receive a fresh dose of joy today. Decide in your heart to trust God fully with every hope and dream you possess. Refuse the bait of offense, discouragement, or disappointment, and instead, grab hold of God's promises to you. Focus your eyes up on the very real and specific purpose of your life. Feel His word come alive in you in a way that calls you out of the boat, over the mountain, and into your next place of promise. Jesus wants you to walk with Him and share His love. Have a joy-filled day today! Today is the day to have a faith filled day and be close to your family and friends.

OCTOBER 16

It's easier said than done. This phrase "let go and let God," may it take on a Kingdom level definition for you. Learn to rest while He works on your behalf. Understand your role in this Kingdom story and do only what He tells you to do and walk where he leads you to go. Live free from the bondage of others' opinions so you're free to love them the way Christ does. Others will be drawn to your purpose-filled heart that they come to know Jesus for themselves. May your life shine so others may see.

OCTOBER 17

May God release a fresh favor over your life today. He will open doors of opportunity and connect you with people who see what He sees in you! Respond to the gentle whisper of His Spirit and go where He sends you. Rely on His voice to take you to your next place of promise. Allow Him to refine your character and redefine what 'success' is supposed to look like for you. Find joy and fulfillment in your work; find peace in your rest; and be fruitful in everything you put your hand to. You are a divinely anointed, appointed, child of Almighty God. Walk in faith every step of the way!

OCTOBER 18

May God Himself pour out His Spirit on you and every member of your family! You and everyone you know can experience God's love more deeply and profoundly. Allow his healing in you, your mind, your body and in your spirit! God will awaken your faith, engage your heart, and empower your prayers. Begin to see what He wants you to see, say what He wants you to say, and pray what He wants you to pray. You belong to Him. You are His ambassador on the earth today. He is good. His promises are true, and He will make a way for you. Lift your hands in praise for all He's done and all He's about to do. He is always good, and you are always loved.

OCTOBER 19

May you find a new freedom in being the you God created you to be! Be comfortable in your own skin, excited about your own story, and at peace with your own past because Christ has redeemed every part of you. You can break free from condemnation, you can walk away from toxic influences, and you can put fear under your feet. Let faith fill your heart. Do not give people the power that belongs to God alone. He loves you. He is strong. And He'll keep you strong to the end. Have a faith-filled day!

OCTOBER 20

May this your next chapter of your life be one of Rest, Revival, and Renewal. Experience the REST of God in your most trying circumstances; and as a result, find peace and bear fruit where's there's only been angst and thorns. Experience a personal REVIVAL that changes how you pray, what you say, and where you put your time. Experience such soul RENEWAL that even the old things in your life feel new. God doesn't make things "nice." He makes things "new." Trust Him to do a brand-new work in you in the days ahead.

OCTOBER 21

May you determine to be done with captivity. No more rehearsing your failures or rehashing your critics' accusations. It's time to remember God's love, His faithfulness, and His heart of affection for you. It's time to put all of your hope in the finished work of Jesus Christ. Put a flag in the ground this day and declare, "My hope is built on nothing less but Jesus's blood and righteousness!" Rest in God's grace. Rely on His love. Rehearse His promises because they're true for you. Break free from the bondage of others' opinions and walk free and full of faith today!

OCTOBER 22

May God surprise you with moments of grace and refreshment. He will bring the long-awaited breakthrough. He will you with sudden belly laughter and watery eyed joy. Allow Him to give you a gift that you least expect. He will inspire you to pray more audaciously than you ever have before. He is with you and for you. No matter what you're going through, may you remember that your identity is secure in Christ; it's not up for grabs or changeable with popular opinion. Jesus is sold on the idea of you and loves how He made you. Trust Him to guide, provide, correct, and redirect you along the way. Love people but keep your hope in the Lord. With eyes of faith find a reason for hope. Seasons come and seasons go, but God's love for you is abundant, profound, and amazingly real, right here, right now. Walk like you're loved because you are beyond your wildest dreams.

OCTOBER 23

May the Lord pour out a fresh anointing on your life today! Allow Him to revive your heart, refresh your soul, and replenish your storehouses. Allow Him to fill you with overflowing and spilled over blessings. Feel His healing in the deep places in your soul. He will reveal where you're vulnerable to the enemy's schemes. He will help you shore up your life so that you can stand strong in the stormy seasons. He is with you. He is for you. Open your hands and receive what He has for you today. And may His joy put a spring in your step!

OCTOBER 24

May God revive your heart for earnest, consistent prayer. Remember once again that God moves on every act prompted by your faith. Rejoice in the fact that God keeps His promises and answers prayers. Even though you can't see it yet, He's created a stream in the desert for you. He's made a way where there's been no way. Soon, you will see the breakthrough, which will compel you to pray more fervently with humble, bold faith, and more specifically with your eyes on His promises. So, rejoice today! Pray today! Believe today! You have a God who is mighty to save. He's the God of the breakthrough! Don't give up hope! Keep on praying. Keep on believing!

OCTOBER 25

May you bend your ear toward heaven and listen to Jesus's words over you, they are healing, redemptive, and life-giving. Bend your ear away from negative words, opinions, and comments. When you're tempted to listen to contrary voices, allow God's truth to fill your heart and drown out lesser opinions. Decide your words will be encouraging, positive, and uplifting. It costs zero to be kind. You are made in God's image for a divine purpose on the earth today. Even your battles can serve you well if you trust God to train you in them. Nothing can separate you from His great love for you. He has set His affection on you and He's not giving up on you! Choose faith in this place today. Wrap your arms around this truth: God is with you and it's impossible for Him to fail you! Lean into Jesus today. He's got you.

OCTOBER 26

As the day begins, may you embrace God's grace, trusting He'll fill every gap. Instead of being unsettled by your imperfections, be assured by Jesus's perfect love for you. Instead of fretting over your mistakes, rejoice that He will never leave your side. Scoop this day into your hand, embrace it, and lift it up as an offering to the One who moves mountains and performs miracles, with every little handful we give Him. He's a miracle working God, He loves you and is for you!

OCTOBER 27

May you pause today and reflect on the wonder of what it means to have Christ in you! Feel His peace abide in you and allow it to restore your soul. His healing will come alive in you and make you whole. Feel His strength rise up in you and make you strong! Allow His love to overwhelm you and fill your heart with a new song. His life in your life changes everything. He's holding you and promises to never let you go. When your arms get tired, rest in His, because it's His strong arms that will sustain you. He loves you, He's in you, so you have all you need. Rejoice in the wonderful reality of Christ in you! A blessed and beautiful day to you this day!

OCTOBER 28

May God's opinion matter far more to you than man's opinion. May His dreams for you speak louder than your fears. Refuse to read into situations that make you anxious. Jesus's promise to protect and provide will be enough for you. His forgiveness will wash over every sin from your past. You will rise up in the knowledge that He's made you brand new, through and through. No spot or stain on you! Don't be afraid to dream that dream, don't be afraid to take a chance. May you remember, He put the dream in you, He gave you the ability to step out in faith. Whatever He has appointed, He has anointed.

OCTOBER 29

Can you hear that? Can you sense He is near? May you dare to scoot a little closer to Jesus, cup your ear, and listen to what He has to say to you. May you take a chance, zone into what He is saying to you today. He loves you. He cherishes you. He has hopes for you. He wants to heal you, restore you, and renew you. His truth will set you free. His power will part the waters. His love will heal your soul. His heart for you will make you whole. Lean in today. Listen for His voice; it's gentle, powerful, redemptive, and life-giving. Oh, how He loves you! I double dog dare you to believe...you can be so much more in Him than you can imagine right here, right now. Dare to believe!

OCTOBER 30

May you experience a personal revival that forever marks the way you walk with God. Seek to have your loved ones encounter Him in ways that change how they pray, what they say, and how they live. God will move on your prayers in ways that compel you to pray more specifically, with greater fervency, and with increasing faith. Though the enemy is working overtime, he runs scared when God steps in. Allow God to move mightily in our midst in the days ahead!

OCTOBER 31

May you learn to rest in the finished work of Christ. Refuse to let your emotions dictate your perspective. You have Jesus. You have His presence. And you have His promises! When what your eyes see is different than what your heart deeply desires, look up and pray. He invites you to walk with Him, talk with Him, and involve Him in every detail of your life. If you're in the "not-yet" season, take time to worship God because He's God; take time to thank Him too, because He's been good. And dare to ask for the impossible because He's a wonder-working God. Your story is not over yet. Others may know your name, but not your story. May you never let fear overtake as you share your story. Your story may be the open book that someone else needs to read to bring them closer to Him. Never fear the "not yet" season.

DON'T LOSE FOCUS.

DON'T LOSE HOPE.

ALWAYS REMEMBER,

YOUR STORY IS STILL BEING WRITTEN.

Write Notes:

__/__/__

November

NOVEMBER 1

May God give you faith to put fear under your feet. Know that for every way the enemy comes against you, the Lord has a promise to bless you, empower you, and to help you stand strong. Fix your eyes on Jesus and set your heart on His word. Know this: when the enemy comes in like a flood, the Lord will raise up a standard against him! Trust in God, raise your shield, and walk forward in faith! Blessings today as you walk in faith!

NOVEMBER 2

May you believe that your wildest God-given dreams can come true. Trust Jesus enough to follow Him through the valley to lay hold of them. Be patient and purposeful. Command your selfish ambition die, and your holy ambition arise. Lean into your training time so you'll be prepared and strengthened to stand in your next place of promise. You know that you'll be poised to change the world. Rest in Him, find your place in Him, trust your dreams to Him. Have a blessed and dream-filled day!

NOVEMBER 3

God is everywhere. God waits on us. As if we are at a picnic table, waiting patiently for a family, a couple, or a single person to come dine; that's how it is with God. He is sitting, waiting patiently for us to come and dine at the Master's Table. The difference in the lone picnic table is we would come to it and spread our food preparations. However, God has prepared for us the most delicious banquet, all we have to do is "show up." No preparations, just come as we are. In this disgruntled, disillusioned and hungry world…God is waiting to give us a banquet of love, peace, comfort, hope, and grace. Enjoy your banquet of blessings today!

NOVEMBER 4

May God do a brand-NEW thing in and through you! He will break every generational stronghold that keeps you from knowing and experiencing His great love for you. He will move every mountain that blocks your view of Him. Allow Him to fill every low place with pools of blessings. He wants to restore everything stolen so you can have the life He intended for you from the beginning of time. Your Redeemer is strong and mighty, and He loves you deeply. Live joyfully today!

NOVEMBER 5

No one expects the rug to be yanked out from under them; life-changing events usually don't announce themselves. While instinct and intuition can help provide some warning signs, they can do little to prepare you for a feeling of rootlessness that follows when fate flips your world upside down. Anger, confusion, sadness, and frustration are shaken up together inside you like a snow-globe. It takes years for the emotional dust to settle as you do your best just to see through the storm. May you be assured when life takes those twists and turns and your stomach feels in knots, God is still with you. When the world is uncertain and life feels hopeless, God is still in control. When your "secured" job is no longer feeling so secure, God is your source. When family and friends turn against you, God is your comfort and best friend. May you be assured when life feels like a roller coaster ride, God is still with you. Be assured when you feel like you're sinking in the depths of despair, God is still with you. Be assured when we feel like you can't crawl out of the quicksand of hopelessness, God is still with you. Focus on Him, turn your eyes to the promises He has made and be assured God is still with you. Have a focused, hope-filled day today!

NOVEMBER 6

Whether you're in the valley, on a mountain or feeling like you're on an endless road, may you remember most importantly that as a Christ-follower you are seated with Him in heavenly realms. Everything He has is yours. He's written your name on His hand and holds your desires close to His heart. Though the elements rage on earth, your footing is secure in Him. Stay hidden in the shelter of His wing; stay in that place of peace. Nothing can separate you from His powerful, personal love for you. You're everything to Him. Look up, enjoy the beautiful view He created just for you!

NOVEMBER 7

May you see the wisdom and power of entrusting your cares to God. When you bow low, He rises up! He will deliver, defend, and establish you. In the meantime, may you learn to rest in His care, trust in His word, and embrace a joy-filled life. Jesus knows your name, has your address, and loves you right here, right now. He will get you where you need to go. He will reach out to the ones you love. He will validate and vindicate you at the proper time. Allow yourself to see and believe that you're safest when you're at His feet, trusting Him to do what you cannot do for yourself. Your soul will find rest in Him. He's got you. Have a trust-filled day!

NOVEMBER 8

He is the Way that will see you through suffering. His word has been proven tried and true. His word is truth, which will never lead us astray. His word will make a way when there seems to be no way. He is the life. He gives us hope in the middle of suffering. He transforms our lives. Cultivate a lifestyle that creates space for grace, growth, and transformation. A complete metamorphosis of every part of your life. Guard against toxic thoughts, attitudes, and mindsets that only weaken you. Fill your thoughts with all that's lovely, praiseworthy, truthful, and life filled. In the days ahead, find joy in your intimate walk with Jesus form your decisions, renew your prayers, and exemplify your love. Guard your thoughts, focus and hide His words in your heart and it'll change your life. We are on an ongoing transformation...always progressing. Take one step at a time, He's got you!

NOVEMBER 9

May Jesus increase His territory through you! Allow Him more access to your soul, more influence in your life, and more voice in your choices. When you come to the edges of yourself and you're hemmed in by your own humanity, don't despair, rejoice! There's more of Jesus for you! The enemy of your soul wants you to focus on your disappointments and limitations. The Savior of your soul wants you to look up, trust Him, and believe Him for great things. Don't let your heart be troubled. Jesus answers prayers and He will profoundly love the world through you! Be kind, show His grace today!

NOVEMBER 10

Scripture says that the same power that raised Christ from the dead is alive and available to us! Allow the power of the risen Christ within you, quicken your mortal body, and make you strong. Feel His love overwhelm you and fill you with joy. Allow His passion for the lost, overtake you and change how you view people. Seek His endless resources and promises that will provide change on how you give and live. In every way, begin to live out of the divine supply offered you by Christ today. Live the other-worldly life He's promised you. You are so precious to Him. Have a bold, powerful, faith-filled day today!

NOVEMBER 11

May you understand, on an entirely different dimension, just how much on your side God is. Open your eyes and see wonders unfold before you that remind you how much it matters that you pray. Plant new seeds of faith, expectant that you'll see a harvest in the days to come.

Take faith steps even if you don't feel like it. Yes, it's okay to cry and Yes, it's okay to laugh. Invite God to heal a deep soul wound that has plagued you for far too long. Take new land with expectant faith. Be strong in the Lord and the power of His mighty love.

NOVEMBER 12

Life throws many curves—whether it's the loss of a job or health due to the ongoing global pandemic, we've just experienced. It may be the uncertainty, and even loss of a marriage or relationship issues, problems with children, and so many other issues that can, and will occur at some point during our life's journey. It could be the unprecedented racial and political unrest. God wants to give us the confidence, He is still with us. So many times, we are afraid to lay ourselves open to others because of historical hurts and emotional injuries. God is still with us even when we feel broken, alone, forsaken, and uncertain about our futures—even our present circumstances. But God will never disappoint. He will never cause disillusionment or discouragement. He is our best source of support if we allow Him to be so. Don't allow anyone else the pen to write your story. Take today and begin trusting Him for more than you've ever begun to imagine. He will never disappoint. Blessings!

NOVEMBER 13

The veil between heaven and earth seem especially thin. Allow yourself sense, like never before, the presence and the power of the living God. Jesus won the victory. He defeated death and sin. He made a public spectacle of the powers that oppose us. Though you have troubles and trials, you serve a strong and mighty God who means what He says and does what He says He'll do. One day there'll be no more tears; no more war; no more hatred. Keep walking. Keep believing because you're only passing through. You're heaven bound. Live like it's true today and every day. Have a most blessed day!

NOVEMBER 14

As you walk forward to your next place of promise, refuse the bait of discouragement, offense, or fear. Instead, walk forward in faith, full of hope, and rich in love. Be sensitive to God's voice that you rest when He says rest and run when He says run. He knows what's best for you and He'll get you where you need to go. Stay focused, prayerful, and hopeful. Though there are giants in the land, you have God on your side. Be brave. Be strong. Be courageous. He's got you.

NOVEMBER 15

Throw caution to the wind? Remember when you used to forgive yourself more quickly for not always being perfect. You can get that back again. You really can. That doesn't have to mean letting people down or walking away. It just means being kinder to you, feeling brave enough to say no sometimes. Being brave enough to stop sometimes and rest. It starts the moment you realize that you're not quite who you used to be. Some of that is good, some of that is not. There are parts of you that need to be brought back. If anyone in your life is not okay with that, they are not your people. Your people will be glad to see that spark starting to light up again. So, if you have been slowly fading away my friend, this is the time to start saying yes to things that bring you joy and no to things that don't. Focus on Him. Focus on His goodness. Let the bravado rise up within you. You can do this. Yes, you can!

NOVEMBER 16

May you understand, on a whole new level, how God is for you. Look and see wonders unfold before you that remind you how much it matters that you pray and believe. Plant new seeds of faith, expectant that you'll see a harvest in the days to come. Take faith steps even if you don't feel like it. Invite God to heal a deep soul wound that has plagued you for far too long. It's a brand-new day! His mercies are fresh, morning-by-morning. Have expectant faith for a bigger and brighter future. May you keep focused on the present and future, not on the past. Be strong in The Lord and the Power of His Might, today and the days ahead!

NOVEMBER 17

Have you ever heard the phrase "when life gives you lemons, make lemonade?" I have many times, especially when there is a situation you're facing, and someone just doesn't have the words to say. Well, today may you especially be able to hear the voice of God reassuring you that lemons have a purpose as well. May you realize with the hardships come blessings. When all the world appears against you, He is for you. When there is destruction, there is a rebuilding. When there are ashes, beauty will rise from those ashes. I challenge you today, grab some lemons, make some lemonade, and wrap yourself in His word. Blessings to you, my friend.

NOVEMBER 18

May the Lord Himself open your eyes and awaken your heart to the truth about who you are from HIS perspective. In Christ Jesus, you are dearly loved, profoundly called, and divinely equipped. You possess all the riches of heaven. His promises belong to you. Walk and talk and pray and live in a manner worthy of your royal status in Him. Believe with your whole heart that YOU are positioned right where you are, for such a time as this. Allow God increase your influence, anoint your words, and appoint your everyday moments. You're a royal ambassador for the Most High God. When you feel like you are standing alone, look around—you are surrounded by His presence.

NOVEMBER 19

Not all storms come to disrupt your life, some come to clear your path. Let go of the illusion that it could have been different, because there are some things we only learn through a storm. The storm is sent to keep us intact with God and to stable our relationship with HIM. Also, He prunes us from every doubtful behavior and thoughts. God wants us to trust Him and to be at peace, even when the storm rages. Many times, when the storm roared and you almost drowned, allow God to rescue you and you re-blossomed through it so many times. People around can smell the rain of restoration in you. So don't give up, don't quit so easily. Be bold, keep Christ your center each day. God will sustain you and bring you through brighter, like a shining star. He will demolish the plans of the enemy and restore everything in double portions you have lost! Believe and have faith in God! Keep trusting him and be humble, in due season He will exalt you.

NOVEMBER 20

One day, you will share your story. The story of how you overcame whatever you are going through right here, right now. Your story will become part of someone else's survival guide. I've always said you can never take someone where you've never been. At the time you are in survival mode, not realizing someone will come into your life whom you will help. You will be able to help them because you will be able to share how God brought you through. May you never be afraid to share your story. May you realize, it truly will help someone along the way.

November 21

Have you ever for no apparent reason completely forgotten what you were getting ready to say? Forgotten what you were going into the kitchen for? Stress will cause us to lose focus, quickly and easily. It's easy to say...Don't lose focus...Don't lose hope. It's another thing altogether to have experienced lost focus. God has good things ahead when we realize He is still in control, no matter how often stressors cause us to lose focus. Remember your journey is for a purpose and if we never experience trials, we can't help others through theirs. May you allow the Glory of Him to shine through you.

November 22

May we pray and believe! Today, Lord Jesus, glorify Your Name in me. In my wins and my losses, in my heartaches and my joys. Be the song of my heart and the reason that I sing. Lift me up so I can see things from Your perspective. Strengthen me to stand right here, right now, while I wait for my breakthroughs and celebrate my victories. You are alive in me. My heart cannot even fathom the good things You have in store for me. Help me to live with my spirit-eyes open so that my heart beats in rhythm with Yours. Any gift from Your hand pales in comparison to know Your heart. You're my greatest treasure and

I embrace wholehearted faith. I will remember, even in the middle of change and uncertainties, you are still Sovereign! You still Reign Supreme. Your plans are so advanced and futuristic, I can't always see Your working on our behalf, but by my faith, you are my strength today. I pray, I believe, I receive your strength today!

NOVEMBER 23

My husband shared a message many years ago entitled "If God brought you to it, He will get you through it." I'll never forget at that time, many were facing the housing crisis, bank failures, and an economy that was uncertain to say the least. During those times, I watched the faithful remain certain of their future in Him. It seems the same times are on us again. May you allow His spirit to give you a sense of calm, even when the world is crashing around you. May you allow Him to show you just how mighty He is on your behalf. May others see your blessed life because you've remained steadfast and solid in your faith. Stay focused, stay faithful.

NOVEMBER 24

On the eve of Thanksgiving Day, set aside your fears, worries, and frustrations, and pull close the ones you love. Savor every bite of nourishment God provides. Notice sacred moments and give thanks for all that is right in your world, even though everything may not be perfect. May the Lord make Himself especially real to you in the coming days. Grow in your capacity to thank Him and trust Him. Family and friends are important, cherish them...time is too short and life is precious. Overlook the things that irritate, appreciate the uniqueness of how God created each of us. Enjoy your holiday, by giving Thanks with a grateful heart.

NOVEMBER 25

The Thanksgiving holiday can bring many emotions, both positive and negative. On this holiday, choose the positive news of JOY-HOPE-FRIENDSHIP-THANKFULNESS. Thanksgiving can be so different without sharing it with loved ones, family, and friends. Families can't spend every holiday together, but always make an effort to be together in heart and spirit. Never waste a moment, call your friends and family. Let them know you love and care. Life is too short. Count your blessings, and the blessings of family. Stretch out your arms, open your hands, and receive a fresh dose of joy today. Decide in your heart to trust God fully with every hope and dream you possess. Open your eyes to the very real and specific call on your life. Allow His word to come alive in you in a way that calls you out of the boat, over the mountain, and into your next place of promise. Seek to learn how you should walk with Him and share His love. During this holiday, as you gather with others of different opinions and beliefs, be the light of Christ.

NOVEMBER 26

May God open your spirit-eyes to see your life, your worth, and your destiny from His point of view. He's doing a beautiful work in you. Open wide your arms and receive His abundant love, His powerful promises, and His moment-by-moment faithfulness. He will not fail you. Live as one who is spoken for, provided for, and deeply loved. Because you are. Take a moment and reflect on how He has blessed you and who He allows you to share those blessings with. Reflect upon your blessings and those wonderful friends and family He has placed in your life. Though things may look different, appear different, and even are different this year, allow Him to continue in you what He desires for you. Believe Him for all things in your life.

NOVEMBER 27

When you step back and survey the parts of your life that break your heart or the things that don't make sense right now, dare to stand strong, look up, and consider what God's resurrection power can do in, through, and around you! Only those who've walked through the valley of the shadow will truly grasp the power of redemption on the other side. Jesus withholds no good thing from those who walk intimately with Him. He's not the reason you suffer; He's with you in the storm. He is your Shelter, Deliverer, and Strong Tower. He's Your Redeemer, Savior, and Friend. He's your Prince of Peace and Sure Defender. Find your footing again. Engage your faith. Embrace a right perspective. Trust Jesus with your whole heart and see what Love will do.

NOVEMBER 28

May the Lord enlarge your territory, expand your influence, and increase your capacity to walk in faith. Allow His hand of power be upon you in a way that marks everything you do. He will keep you from harm—both causing and enduring it—and He will use you to bless a world very much in need. He will surprise you with breakthroughs an still-water- refreshing moments. Walk forward unafraid with the full knowledge that your Shepherd goes before you. He's placed His hand of blessing upon your head, and He will faithfully lead you. Have a lighthearted, joy-filled day today!

NOVEMBER 29

Have you ever sat on the edge of your seat, heart pounding, and nerves on edge while watching your favorite sports team? I sure have. When the missed field goal would've determined the game. When a clutch-buzzer-beater basket determines the outcome. At the end of it all, it's still a game. May we realize this thing called life is not a game. May we realize we need Him more and more as the days and years progress on our life journey. May we allow Him to be our confident assurance, when it looks like we can't prevail—He will on our behalf.

NOVEMBER 30

Can you hear that? Lean in, can you hear the quiet whisper of His voice? May you take moments to pause today and listen for God's gentle whisper in your ear. May today be the day, you fully respond to that slightest nudge of the Spirit within you and do the next thing God gives you to do. May today be the day you refuse to get your perspective from the surface appearance of things. Pause, lean in, and listen for The Lord in this place. He has something for you here; something you need to take with you to your next place of promise. Remember that in every single step of the way, you are His. He's got you. Have a wise, lean-in-to-His-voice kind of day today!

DON'T LOSE FOCUS.

DON'T LOSE HOPE.

ALWAYS REMEMBER,

YOUR STORY IS STILL BEING WRITTEN.

Write Notes:

--/--/--

Write Notes:

__/__/__

December

December 1

May Jesus lift your chin today and speak life into your weary soul. Remember how much He loves you. Your bumps and bruises will be healed in His presence. Shake off yesterday's frustrations and tomorrow's worries, and rest in the reality of His divine involvement in your life. Jesus is more than enough for you. Listen for His life-giving invitation to you. He invites you to rest with Him. You are loved, treasured, appointed, and anointed. You're free to climb mountain heights with joy and free to stumble and fall without condemnation. Jesus holds you and will lead you safely home. Know His love. Trust His heart. Be yourself. And do only what He asks you to do. Have a heart-at-rest sort of day today!

December 2

May you allow Jesus to lead you to edges of your comfort zone and give you a fresh vision for where He's taking you. Put everything on the table and give Him permission to rearrange your life. Dare to open your hands, look up, and breathe a prayer of thanks right in the midst of this uncertain time, knowing that He's far kinder than you can fathom and far greater than you ever imagined. He has given us the owners' manual, read it—use it—live it. Answer Jesus's invitation to join Him on this adventure of faith. It's our free-will choice, choose Him. Will you trust Him? Choose joy! God wants to do a deep and profound work in and through you! Your security is found in Him! Have a blessed, peace-filled day.

December 3

May you refuse an anxious heart and embrace a faith-filled one. Stomp on your fears and dance because of your dreams. Disregard the shame of your youth and hold tight your new identity in Christ. You're not an improved version of your old self. You're something altogether new, profoundly beautiful, and abundantly equipped. Walk fully in the blessing and purposes of God today.

December 4

May you know—in the deepest places of your soul—that Jesus is working in ways you cannot see. In due time your faith will become sight and you'll be glad that you trusted Him. Trust that He's working on your behalf. And in the meantime, be generous to those in need, compassionate to those who struggle, and kind to those whom the world overlooks. You're an ambassador of the Most High God. Trust Him with your whole life, period. Have a joyfully blessed day!

December 5

May God give you deep and nourishing assurance today. He has your situation under control. Nothing happens that He can't handle on your behalf. Begin your day refreshed and ready to carry God's light and easy yoke for you. Refuse to carry that which He has not assigned. Look up with joy knowing He's with you every step of the way. A blessed day is yours!

DECEMBER 6

May God infuse you with divine energy and purpose today. He will fuel your prayers and sanctify your words. Open your eyes to see evidence of His handiwork everywhere you turn. He will you with people you need to meet. He will connect others with you who need your blessing. Walk with authority, confidence, joy, and strength today. You are mighty in God!

DECEMBER 7

As the winds of change start to blow in your life, lean in and listen for the voice of the Lord. Instead of looking for "signs" and mistakenly drawing the wrong conclusion, look to the Lord and His strength. He'll speak to you in a way you'll understand. He'll lead you in the way you should go. He is faithful and true and He's doing a new thing in your life! Keep an ear bent toward heaven. Daily the heavens pour forth speech. May you listen for every word. Blessings on your life.

DECEMBER 8

May God stir up fresh faith in your heart. Send prayers packed with power and your words seasoned with love. God will give you divine instinct so you're always in the right place at the right time. He will open a door for you no man can close. Recite His promises and rehearse His faithfulness. God is good. Walk forward in faith. Feel God's blessings today!

December 9

May you refuse to drag the heavy baggage from your past another step. Refuse to borrow tomorrow's trouble when it's not yours to carry. Grab a hold of today's mercy, tonight's grace, and the power offered you. Walk in the promised influences God has assigned you. Walk in a manner worthy of His name. Feel confidence and humble dependence on God's word and seek His mark in your life in every way today.

December 10

May you refuse to let your emotions dictate your perspective. You have Jesus. You have His presence. And you have His promises! When what your eyes see is different than what your heart deeply desires, look up and pray. He invites you to walk with Him, talk with Him, and involve Him in every detail of your life. Take time to worship God because He's God; take time to thank Him too, because He's been good. And dare to ask for the impossible because He's a wonder-working God. Your story is not over yet. Have a heart-at-rest kind of day. God bless you!

December 11

May you begin and nurture a lifestyle that allows for times of replenishing rest, powerful prayer, and thoughtful consideration to what God is saying to you in this season. Push away the clutter and treat yourself to some time and space to hear what God has to say to you this day. God is with you. His activity surrounds you. Jesus is near. Yet the culture races on as if He doesn't exist. But He lives! And His promises are true for you. Calm your anxious heart. Trust His love for you. Open your hands and let Him fill them. He gives good gifts to His children. And YOU are someone He treasures. Blessings to you this day!

DECEMBER 12

May the Kingdom, power, and presence of the Living God seem nearer to you now than ever before. Seek understanding of what you possess in Him grow exponentially in the days ahead. See glimpses of glory everywhere. You will be reminded that God is very much at work behind the scenes, answering your prayers, opening doors, and moving mountains. Jesus lives to pray for you and when He prays heaven moves. Rest in faith simply because heaven sings a song over you. God is at work on your behalf, and any day now, you will see Him breakthrough. Don't lose focus on Him when we lose our focus it's easy to lose hope. Blessings to you today.

DECEMBER 13

May you stand strong in the face of enemy threats. Remain confident even when an army rises up against you. Put your flag in the ground and declare that if God is for you, so who can stand against you? Far greater is He who is in you, than he who is in the world. You are God's beloved, and He will guard and guide you, shelter and provide for you, bless and establish you. Jesus loves you and nothing and no one can change His mind about you. Live like you're His, because in Christ Jesus, you're an heir!

December 14

May God's perfect love swallow up every single fear and anxious thought. Allow Jesus to renew your perspective in a way that brings you peace and assurance. Pray that your loved ones find their strength in Christ alone. Know that God will do for you what you cannot do for yourself. Let every moment be filled with grace and peace, healing and rest, perspective and power, and pray this in Jesus's Name. He is with you today and every day!

December 15

May God grant you a fresh perspective of His unlimited supply. Trust Him with your needs and desires. Feel Him breathe fresh life into your soul and fresh power into your dreams. Refuse to let your fears and insecurities speak louder than God's voice. Even as you sleep, may your ears be fine-tuned to Heaven's song over you, for it is redemptive, beautiful, and life giving! Claim it today!

December 16

May you pause long enough to meditate on what God is saying to you in this place among the not-yets and the what-ifs. Do you hear His whisper to be still and trust Him? Dream big dreams in the face of your fears and have the courage to hold your ground when you'd rather run and hide. Have the faith to entrust your heart's desires to a God who is very much involved, very much in control, and very much invested in your life. Remember who you are. Remember whose you are. Don't lose perspective. Don't lose focus. Don't lose hope. Hold on, tight, to faith. Have a blessed day.

DECEMBER 17

Have you ever for no apparent reason completely forgotten what you were getting ready to say? Forgotten what you were going into the kitchen for? Stress will cause us to lose focus, quickly and easily. Stress comes in all shapes, forms, and sizes. Stress of the "perfect holiday," The "perfect party," the "perfect tree." Stress of trying to keep the perfect home, job performance, unrealistic expectations. Don't lose focus...don't lose hope. It's another thing altogether to have experienced lost focus. God has good things ahead when we realize He is still in control, no matter how often stressors cause us to lose focus. Remember your journey is for a purpose and if we never experience trials, we can't help others through theirs. May you allow the Glory of Him to shine through you.

DECEMBER 18

In the days ahead, may God mightily increase your desire for Him! May His hand of power be upon you and His influence increase through you. May He keep you from evil and harm, from both causing and enduring it. May He awaken a fresh passion to dream with Him and walk in faith because of Him! May He give you a strong sense of what He wants to accomplish in and through you in this coming year. He is faithful, He will do it, and HE will finish what He's started. Have a joy-filled day today!

DECEMBER 19

No matter if you're in the valley or on a mountain, may you remember most importantly that as a Christ-follower you are seated with

Christ in the heavenly realms. Everything He has is yours. He's written your name on His hand and holds your desires close to His heart. Though the elements rage on earth, your footing is secure in Him. Stay hidden in the shelter of His wing; stay in that place of peace. Nothing can separate you from His powerful, personal love for you. You're everything to Him. Remember His love today. Don't lose focus. Don't lose hope. Always remember, your story is still being written!

December 20

May your precious heart for Jesus upstage your fears about today, and your worries about tomorrow. May His awesome presence transform you so that the opinions of others lose their hold on you. May God's very real love for you spill out in the way you love others. May the guidance and direction of the Holy Spirit take you where you never thought you'd go and help you accomplish what you never dreamed possible. He's a miracle-working God and He'll do great things in and through you if you dare to trust Him. So, trust Him!

December 21

May you choose to be grateful when you'd rather be grumpy. Today, choose to rejoice in God's goodness when you're tempted to rehearse man's badness. Trust God to fill your empty well. God will soon fill it. Live with the expectation that any day now, the Lord will bring the breakthrough. Know that more rests on God's shoulders than on yours. He's got you. Have a blessed and beautiful day!

DECEMBER 22

May you feel the peace only He can give during the raging storm. Event he winds and sea obey His command. May the peace you experience be a beacon to someone who is struggling during their storm. Even though lightning flashes and the thunder roars, it will not overcome the one who puts their trust in peace maker. He will one day break through and redeem your story. Today, allow Jesus to fill you with a new dose of holy confidence and humble dependence so that when others see your peaceful countenance, they'll be compelled to look up and seek God's intervention in their own story. Have a peace-filled day!

DECEMBER 23

The other night we watched a wonderful movie, It was based on a person's horrific, abusive, and brutal treatment during childhood. Yet, somehow with all he was going through...God was gifting him to be an international blessing. Even though, he was fighting his own demons... he went back "home" to see his parent to settle things. What I received from this was a story of forgiveness, redemption, restoration, and healing. May we realize, we are never too far gone that His love can't reach. May we realize redemption is for us. May we realize, healing comes in many forms. May we see active restoration taking place in relationships. Whatever the circumstance, situation, diagnosis, or feelings of despair...He is with us.

DECEMBER 24

What does Christmas really feel like? Is it about the weather? Snow or no snow? Christmas is a feeling in the heart. Wherever we find ourselves, we can experience that feeling, when we have Christ in our heart, we truly have the "feeling" of Christmas no matter what the weather. We can keep that "feeling" all year, not just when we're trying to make the nice list and avoid the naughty list. As each year can bring uncertainties, loss of friends and family, job losses, business closures, a country in turmoil, heightened concern, insecurities, and even a pandemic of unimaginable consequences, we know that God has remained faithful. So, this Christmas Eve, don't lose focus–don't lose hope, keep that "feeling" in your heart and carry it throughout the next year.

December 25

In this Christmas season, may Christmas miracles break forth in ways that surprise and bless you. Feel salvation spring up all around you! See lives changed, relationships restored, and bodies healed every which way you turn. When God sent Jesus sent His Son to us, God's Kingdom came to earth! Expect what God can and wants to do in your midst rise exponentially. He is a star-breathing, miracle-working, intimately involved God. Bless your day today!

December 26

May you give God full access to your story. Allow Him to correct and redirect, heal and deal, refine and define, whenever it suits Him. He loves you most and knows what's best for you at every given moment. He will lead you in the way you should go. Remember that you're part of a great story God is writing in the world. May you allow only Him to use the pen to write your story. Trust the Lord's work in your life so He can use you in ways beyond your wildest dreams. Lean in and trust Him. He's got you.

DECEMBER 27

As you walk through your everyday life, that has become the temporary "new normal," may you dare to scoot a little closer to Jesus, lean in, and listen to what He has to say to you. He loves you. He cherishes you. He has hopes for you. He wants to heal you, restore you, and renew you. His truth will set you free. His power will part the waters. His love will heal your soul. His heart for you will make you whole. Lean in, listen for His voice—His gentle, powerful, redemptive, and life-giving voice. Oh, how He loves you! Oh, how He loves you and me! May you dare to believe who you can be because of Him. Miracles still happen in the middle of chaos, tragedy, and storms. Have a blessed and beautiful day!

DECEMBER 28

May Jesus put your heart at ease this very moment. May you suddenly know and feel and encounter His peace in a way you never have before. Allow joy spring up in your soul where you've only known worry and frustration. Feel the struggles that have plagued you suddenly seem small in the light of God's very real and personal love for you. Allow Jesus to give you a glimpse of His glory, just enough to remind you that you're not walking this road alone. Though we live by faith and not by sight, it's sometimes good for the soul to see what our heart already knows. God will allow you to see just enough to put your soul at ease and your heart at rest. God is good that way. Trust Him to move in close and be your strength today.

December 29

May you pause to enjoy the sacredness and fullness of the season. God will give you plenty of by-the-tree moments to reflect on His intimate and powerful love for you. Seek to have face-to-face encounters with those you love. Pray that God use you to lift up those bent beneath heavy loads. Receive the gifts He so lovingly wants to give. Cherish every second with the ones you love. You can enjoy the journey because His yoke is easy, and His burden is light. He's always near!

December 30

Today may seem to be the longest journey you've ever taken. It may appear you are walking alone. May you be reassured; you are not alone. He is with you. Grief has many faces, let it work out. God created us with emotions and feelings, He will help us through whatever He allowed us to be brought to. We experience loss in many ways, loved ones who are taken too soon; friendships; loss of a precious pet; loss of a job or a lifelong career. When loss overwhelms is, He is still with us. When the support system has gone to their perspective lives, the doorbell is no longer ringing, and the phone calls have ceased...may you be assured He is, and always will be, your support system. May you be assured, you will get through today, and the days ahead, one-step-at-a-time with Him. He will never leave. May you allow Him to wrap His arms around you.

December 31

Lord, what a week it's been. Mercy, what a few weeks it's been. We can even say what a stressful few months, and year, it's been. Through it all...I've seen His goodness and glory even though we've taken a few arrows that have left us burdened and breathless. Yet, He is still God. He is still on His throne. He will see us through. He will take what the enemy meant for evil and turn it for good. May you hide yourself in the shadow of His wing. Trust, entirely, our soul to Him, knowing He has us on His heart and in His hand. May we rest today in Him. May we be assured; He is still in control. Reach out to someone you haven't talked to in a while. Show kindness. Be an instrument of compassion and caring. As you walk forward to your next place of promise, refuse the bait of discouragement, offense, or fear. Walk forward in faith, full of hope, and rich in love. Stay focused, prayerful, and hopeful. Though there are giants in the land, you have God on your side. Be brave. Be strong. Be courageous. He's got you today and every day of every year.

DON'T LOSE FOCUS.

DON'T LOSE HOPE.

ALWAYS REMEMBER,

YOUR STORY IS STILL BEING WRITTEN.

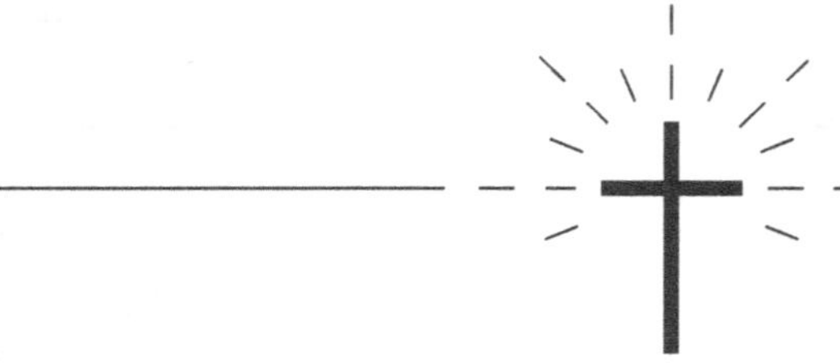

Write Notes:

__/__/__

Write Notes:

--/--/--

Write Notes:

__/__/__

Write Notes:

__/__/__

Write Notes:

__/__/__

Acknowledgments

I would like to acknowledge and thank:

Chris B., who helped me organize my Word documents, and Joel, my photographer.

www.ingramcontent.com/pod-product-compliance
Lightning Source LLC
LaVergne TN
LVHW020045110826
845155LV00029B/633

* 9 7 8 1 9 5 4 9 7 8 9 6 6 *